Somebody is born.
Somebody goes to school.
Somebody learns to conform.
Somebody types a CV.
Somebody gets a job.
Somebody follows orders.
Somebody gets a golden watch.
And then, eventually,
Somebody dies.
And, a Nobody is buried.

THE CONFESSIONS OF A MISFIT

REASONS WHY I SUCK SO MUCH

MOKOKOMA MOKHONOANA

An Occasional Failure™
Non-award-winning Creative
Author of No Bestseller

sekoala
PUBLISHING COMPANY (PTY) LTD

sekoala
PUBLISHING COMPANY (PTY) LTD

ISBN: 978-0-620-48087-1

Cover design: Mokokoma Mokhonoana
Book design: Mokokoma Mokhonoana

Sekoala Publishing Company (Pty) Ltd

www.sekoala.com

"All great deeds and all great thoughts have a ridiculous beginning."

— **Albert Camus**

A Word of Foolishness

So, ... a guy that is a nobody to almost everybody; has two blogs with a collective of three subscribers; foolishly thinks that he can write a book that will leave four million people five times greater, wiser, and with an attitude of gratitude, in less than six readings of a "not-so-categorizable" book filled with his "random opinions."

A guy that has been broke for the most part of his adult life (Thank God for pocket money. Or else, it would have been "... his entire life."), foolishly thinks that he can talk about money, entrepreneurship, passive income, building wealth, and, financial freedom.

A guy that is a few weeks away from celebrating his second anniversary since his relationship status was forced to go from "taken" to "single and ready to mingle," by a not-so-understandable misunderstanding, foolishly thinks that he can give pointers on dating, love, women, relationships, offsprings, family, and, happiness.

Hello, I'm Mokokoma. The foolish guy and I are one.

A Word of Warning

I am more obsessed with how words make a sentence look; than with what the words spell out, convey, or, express. So, ... in almost all cases, sentences look way better than what they communicate.

The ratio of "playfulness" to "seriousness" is about 88 to 1.

All that I'm striving for is to make sense; not to be right. In terms of both opinions and grammar. So, if a sentence with a mispelt word still makes sense; then, correct spelling, in that case, is overrated.

All puns in here are intended, and, all rhymes are by design.

I will not be liable for whatever deeds (or lack thereof) inspired by the writings in this book, esp. parts where I talk about women, resigning, allowing workers to sleep at work, and, self-employment.

Some of the words that I used in here do not really "exist."

I have been called "arrogant," twelve point seven times more than the number of times that I've been referred to as "black", "tall", "normal", "funny", "humble", "sane" and "male," put together.

And oh, I overused the word "overrated."

A Word to the Creators

The very little that I know, and the few things that I excel in doing, are by-products of love, litres of coffee, an extreme obsession with reading, eating "bread and baked beans" daily, sleepless nights, and, 'unceasingly' conquering "the curse of instant gratification."

I have slaved and sacrificed a lot to be what, who, and, where I am.

But, with that said, the biggest slice of the praise that I get for the things that I do or say should go to the Creator. For a great player could have easily been suffocated by the bench; should the coach have not given the player an opportunity to be, do, and, shine.

Moreover, without a "He" and a "She," I would not be.

Mama le Papa, I will not even attempt to express my appreciation for the love, home, wisdom, food, and, pocket money, that you gave me. No elegant font / brilliant writing will be able to capture even a tenth of the gratitude that I have for having been blessed with such loving, wise, supportive, and, funny parents. And, ...

As if that was not enough; you blessed me with Thato le Seforo.

It is either that, or, you blessed them with me. Either way, ... they are the best brother and sister that I could have ever asked for. Ta!

"Mmanoko le Setemere — Ke leboga lerato, ponelo pele, thlokomelo, le gose fele pelo ga lena!"

A Word of Thanks

I would like to thank yesterday's failures for today's successes.

I would like to thank all the challenges, losses, failures, problems, misfortunes, heartbreaks, and, rough patches, that life was kind enough to place on the path of my journey of this, mysterious yet straightforward, sometimes regarded as a bitch, thing called life.

I would like to thank today's losses for tomorrow's gains.

I would also like to thank all the would-have-been my employers; for failing to "see" the genius that was hidden in me.

I would like to thank every single person that I have met, and, ... I would also like to thank every single person that I have never met.

And, last but not least, I would like to thank my father for having the guts to run after my mother, the day that he did. And, equally important, I'd like to thank my mother for not playing hard to get.

... Because of that, I am.

"If everyone is thinking alike,
then somebody isn't thinking."

— **George S. Patton**

The Confessions of a Misfit

REASONS WHY I SUCK SO MUCH

A World of Opinions

"To repeat what others have said requires education; to challenge it requires brains."

— **Mary Pettibone Poole**

The End.

Introduction

"A man is literally what he thinks, his character being the complete sum of all his thoughts." — James Allen, *As a Man Thinketh*.

If a person is indeed what he / she thinks; then the opinions, ideas, quotations, questions, suggestions, experiences, experiments, misconceptions, perceptions, understandings and misunderstandings, found in the pages ahead are to blame for "*why I suck so much.*"

That is, if not "seeing the world" the same way as the rest of the world sees the world means that one sucks, then "I plead guilty."

First thing first, this book is not about one particular subject.

And that's simply because I don't believe that the golfer in a great golfer is solely accountable for the greatness of the golfer. I strongly believe that the friend, the foe, the neighbour, the stranger, the seller, the buyer, the speaker, the listener, the teacher, the learner, the receiver, the giver, the lover, the hater, the ex-lover, the marketer, the consumer, etc. in the golfer, also play an imperative role.

That's to say, the marketer in, say, Nelson Mandela, contributed to his triumph in selling his aspirations to the people of South Africa.

It is plausible to believe that there is a marketer in every one of us.

... Seeing that even a homeless person has to 'sell' their homelessness in a 'compelling' manner; for them to increase the odds of a passerby sparing them a dime or two. Parents too, at some point, have to sell the importance of, say, education, to their kids. And, in most cases, it takes the same principles and creativity to sell, say, one's opinions, as it takes a brand to sell, say, a "bag of onions."

Likewise, there is an imperative need for a marketer in every single prostitute. It's either that or no one will come. Both figuratively and literally. I too will use the marketer in me to 'sell' you my opinions.

1

In this book, I've systematically shared random rants and opinions.

Amongst other things, ... I rant about rent ... friends, trends, rands and brands. Sex and tax. Health and wealth. How-to 'design' and reasons to resign. The middle-class and the foolish things that we were "fed" in class. Minimalism and conformism. Employees and employers. Sellers and "the sold to." Slavery and discovery. White people and black people. Nutrition and prostitution. Pros of having a vision and cons of having a television. The overweight and the underpaid. Puppets and G-strings. Baked beans and 'skinny' jeans.

School taught us to cover up to avert other students from copying our answers, made of our knowledge. But with this book, I would like to achieve the opposite. Give away, or rather, share everything that I have learned about everything that falls under the umbrella of life. For I wish not to take the little that I know to the cemetery.

Truth be told, I am tempted to say that this book is a gift to Thato and Seforo. But, unfortunately for their egos, I have been blessed with love for every single member of the human race. I honestly love every single person in the world; even people that I don't like.

For that reason, this book is the best gift that I can give to anyone that is wise, or foolish, enough to invest a few rands and/or their precious time in this book made of nothing but random opinions.

Like I said, the "playfulness" outweighs the "seriousness."

But hidden within what seems to be 'random rants' are principles that I live by. From the decision process of whether or not to enter- tain a woman that was woman enough to confess her love for me; ... to which visual elements to 'discard' when I design, say, a logo.

Figuratively, this book is about three times its literal size.

One writing will mean one thing to one reader; and another thing to another reader. Because the value that you will get out of these writings is highly dependent on how deep you are willing to think.

A writing about, say, dating, might have an invaluable marketing insight hidden within it; and a design principle might be applied to one's way of running, say, a law firm, or their bewildering love life.

Almost all writings in here are metaphorical. That is to say, I wrote about issues that I was not really speaking about. While speaking about issues that I did not really write about. Think of the writings as veggies covered with chocolate to lure you. The nutrients of the veggies (writings) will only nourish (stimulate, enrich, etc.) the bodies (minds) of those who bite (think) deeper than (beyond) the chocolate (metaphors). Don't just read the lines. Read between them.

(I just used a metaphor to tell you that I used a lot of metaphors.)

I strongly believe that this book will "add value" to your life. Irrespective of your age, interests, occupation, maths marks, gender, height, weight, race, religion, geographic location, the depth of your pockets, or, the number of times that you have failed to fail.

Through going through this book: some readers will 'awaken' the genius in them, and, inevitably, some will quit their "secure jobs."

~~Apologies to their employers.~~ Congratulations to such employees.

I insist that everyone is a genius at something. And with this book, all that I am trying to say is that I really don't have a problem with a bird that settles for walking; so long as it is aware that it can fly.

Almost all rants appears to be about "... me, me, me ..." I actually find that a bit boring. But that's the best way that I'm able to share the little that I know. So, I'll mostly talk about me, my opinions, and, my experiences. But it's all for your benefit. Remember, the spoken was known by the speaker before the speaker spoke.

It goes without saying that this is a strange book. But in our world where everybody is trying to be like everybody, strange is valuable.

I took 44 weeks off work, to write this book. But I hope that it will instill an attitude of gratitude, nonconformity, positivity, remarkableness, and, imprint insights that will last for whatever number of years, months, weeks, days, or minutes, that is left of your life.

The Imperfection of Perfection

Perfection is a state of being sought after by many; especially those of us who create. Ironically, it is the main reason (or rather: excuse) why most creators do not get around to ship, publish, or, launch.

Without a doubt, you would not be reading this book right now, should I too have been foolish enough to seek "perfection."

As it happens, this book would have been one of countless ideas that their conceivers took to the graveyard. All thanks to procrastination that is "excused" by the conceiver's pursuit for perfection.

... show me a creation whose creator assuredly regard as perfect; and I will gladly show you a creator living in a fool's paradise — or better still — a fool living in a creator's paradise.

(I actually pray that, while reading this book, you detect a defect.)

There Will Only Be One Tiger in the Woods

Regardless of how much of an "exceptional and talented" golfer you might be; you'll never be Tiger Woods, or, "the next" Tiger Woods. Even if you are, without a doubt, a better golfer than him.

While it is understandable for you to be inspired by Tiger Woods; it is foolish for you to let your obsession with "The world's number one golfer's" greatness push you to try to "be like" Tiger Woods.

The next thing we know, you start sleeping around, with the hope of "improving" your par; even though that rarely gets people far.

But here's a consolation prize: Tiger Woods too, can never be you.

The good thing about being yourself is that it is effortless to be; as opposed to trying to be someone, or something, that you are not.

"Be yourself. Everyone else is already taken."
— Oscar Wilde

(Ahem, I am aware that we could do without the part about adultery and improving pars; but I really have a weakness for rhymes.)

Tomorrow is an illusion

Tomorrow, the day after today, is without a doubt, the most overworked — and poisonous — word in a procrastinator's vocabulary.

I would also like to credit 'tomorrow' as the reason our forefathers spent most part of their lives merely existing; as opposed to living. Owning to the fact that they worked terribly hard in pursuit of a financially secure tomorrow, at the expense of their then "today."

We, as a people, get so caught up in working for a better tomorrow. We blindly follow the "To live like a king, you must work like a slave ..." saying; we sacrifice today, the present, as a result, we fail to realize that in between life, the journey between birth and death, one can only exist within "today," the present, the now.

Being is divisible into three junctures: the past, the present, and the future. But today, the now, is all that was, is, and, will forever be. Today exists, while yesterday, and, tomorrow are all in one's mind.

The two are nothing but abstract references to either: the previous set of twenty-four hours, or the following set of twenty-four hours.

"Tomorrow" is nothing but a term used to refer to a set of twenty-four hours that follows the current set. Tomorrow is a continuously moving target, seeing that, when one is a nanosecond away from reaching "tomorrow" — it is, all of a sudden, called "today."

Tomorrow is like "there." Once you get "there," it's called "here."

So regardless of where one goes, one will forever be within 'here.' Likewise, for as long as you exist, it'll forever be now, thus, today.

The world referred to today as tomorrow, yesterday. Thus, it was, is, and it will forever be, today. Now, the present, is all we will have.

Some philosopher once asked, "If yesterday, and, tomorrow exist, where are they now?" ... I think his question remains unanswered.

(The only day that's worth worrying over is 'today.' For it always is, and, it will forever be. So, only worry about tomorrow, tomorrow.)

Life is Too Short

As undesirable as it is; you don't have forever to do, say, or create all that you desire to. And, what I hate about "forever," is that it is impractical to prove; because it will take forever, to prove 'forever.'

The sad reality is that you 'might' not even get to live long enough to read all of what's left of this book. It's disturbing, ...but 'tis true.

The fact that you saw the last twenty years does not "guarantee" that you will live to see the next coming twenty seconds. I call that The f.Law of Statistics. In that case, studying yesterday is useless.

Exploit the obnoxious fact that sooner or later you're going to kick the bucket. Make use of this inevitable law of life. Use it as an antidote for procrastination; a poison that we're often injected with by our fear of failure and our pursuit for perfection: an illusional state.

I am "inspired" by life, but, I am "motivated" by death.

Life is full of varying kinds of inspirational things; and people. Find them. Be inspired to do, say, or create. And then, use the fact that you don't have forever to do, say, or, create — as a motivation to start doing or creating. Most people think that they are somehow immune to death; even people who have 'lost' a lot of loved ones.

(Er, ... I know that, like most people, you are probably tempted to ask, "Life is too short?! Compared to what?" to anyone that asserts such an axiom about life. Well, the answer is simple. Death.)

"Impossible" is a Temporary Opinion

Is it "possible" for a man, or a woman, to go for a day "without" breathing at all? Is it "possible" for a six-year-old to start with college and still get to pass every single test that is thrown her way?

Is it "possible" for you to make whatever that your employer earns on a good month, on a bad day? Is it "possible" for some random poverty-stricken 'unschooled' kid from Africa to start a cola brand that'll give Coca-Cola's shareholders a good run for their money?

Is it "possible" for a ten-year-old to found a portable media player brand that will be so successful that it leaves Steve Jobs "jobless"?

Well, a day before one of the Wright brothers' untold attempts was successful, transporting people through the air was "impossible."

A day before Henry Ford shamed his critics; making low-cost automobiles was "impossible." A day before Thomas Edison succeeded in creating a light bulb that worked, they too were "impossible."

"Conversing" with someone who is on the other side of the world, without having to write, and post, a letter was "impossible."

Well, ... that was until Alexander Graham Bell, gave us a Tel.

We, as a people, have a "silly," crippling, pathetic, and, disgusting habit of using the word "impossible" instead of "... very difficult."

(Well, to me, "impossible" merely means never done, or seen, before. Therefore, "impossible" is nothing but a temporary opinion.)

Job Security is a Fantasy

It goes without saying that the recession left a lot of "innocent" employees jobless. In some cases, things got worse. Some also lost "their" houses. The downturn left some "homeowners" homeless.

But in there lies a lesson. A lesson that this thing called a "secure" job is nothing but an illusion built by a lot of successive paychecks. The truth is that when push comes to shove, your employer will release you from your contract. Whether he is a good person or not.

So, if your employer's business isn't immune to the challenges and the 'uncertainties' of the market in which it trades in; what makes you think that he can certainly guarantee you a "permanent job"?

(Now that you know that 'job security' is an illusion. Go start that business! ... And, who knows? You might end up employing your boss someday; when your boss's bosses are forced to "cut costs.")

"The housewife is an unpaid
employee in her husband's house in
return for the security of
being a permanent employee."

— Germaine Greer

A Simple Recipe for Everlasting Contentment

We all have "excuses" for not being happy. Perhaps you promised yourself to be happy as soon as you get a job that pays you what you deserve; a lover that loves, calls, respects and appreciates you; or — a car that will retire the pedestrian in you. The list is endless.

But for as long as your happiness is attached to, or dependent on, things or other people; the once in a blue moon contentment that you will realize (if you're lucky) will, without doubt, be short-lived.

What will happen to your "happiness," should you lose your other half; if he or she is the 'sole' reason why you are happy? Will your euphoria still be? Should you then be miserable because things did not work out? If you're happy, solely because it is Monday; isn't it 'foolish' for you to expect the happiness to still be, come Tuesday?

Whatever it is that you are "chasing," things that you refuse to be happy 'until' you get; just know that there are gazillions of people who had a hundred times more of what you are chasing. But they are no more. Chasing money? The cemetery is overpopulated with hundreds and thousands of billionaires. Not happy merely because you're single? Well, I know a dead polygamist. He left eight wives.

The best gift, in life, is life. The problem is that we are so 'used to' being alive, that we fail to appreciate being alive. We momentarily appreciate life when we are told of other people's passing. A few weeks later, we start complaining about not having shoes to wear.

The only thing that you should "attach" your happiness to, is your heartbeat. For it signals, life, the greatest gift of them all. The one thing that I like about such an attitude; is that the only time that you will get to be "unhappy," is when the heartbeat is "no more."

(But then again, ... you would be "too dead" to be "unhappy.")

Knowledge is Not Power

To most people, ... to be more "powerful," one must know more.

I have lost count of people who keep on enrolling with institutions hoping that their newly acquired "knowledge" (qualification) will help them increase their income, or, make them more "powerful."

... Reality check! To be "knowledgeable" is not to be "powerful." Knowledge is not really power — it just has the "potential" to be.

A gun is not lethal; it has the potential to be. A seed is not a tree; the seed merely has the potential to be a tree. Likewise, love does not really hurt; it has the potential to. Er, ... maybe I'm pushing it!

Anyhow, ... without "action," knowledge is rarely "fruitful."

Without any action ('somebody' pulling the trigger) a firearm will, undoubtedly, fail to realize its full potential; to take someone's life.

"Knowledge" is meant to "empower" the knowledgeable. But its presence makes no difference; if it is not 'utilized' by its possessor.

Without any "action" — a cup, a teaspoon, hot water, a tea bag, sugar, and milk, will be exactly that — "a cup, a teaspoon, boiling water, a tea bag, sugar, and, milk" — instead of a hot cup of tea.

To be knowledgeable is to possess potential power; and not to be "powerful" like school, and, society, "programmed" us to believe.

A man with a Doctorate in Medicine; but who is 'lazy' to practice, thereby, failing to put his knowledge into "practice," is not "powerful." Not by a long shot. He's just yet another "starving" doctor.

(Without action paint fails to realize its potential to be a painting.)

Life Goes On
(It Really Does)

I have a friend named Mojeka Moloto, and, he likes saying, "Life goes on ..." esp. in times when life seems to be "unfair" to him.

He would tell me that he just broke up with a potential-mother-to his-unborn-kids that he so dearly loved, or that he was in a car accident that left his pockets even shallower. But he would, without fail, end the conversation with, "Oh well, ... life goes on!"

He is probably the most "stress-free" person that I have ever met.

(When an "unfortunate" thing happens to you — you can either moan about that something that your moaning will not undo, or better, or you can accept your loss, let it be, and, just be thankful for another "lesson" that life was kind enough to bless you with.)

Kids Aren't Parents' 2nd Chance to
Unrealized Dreams

At times parents push their children to "achieve" what they failed to achieve. What's worse is that some parents still push their children to achieve things that they, themselves, were able to achieve.

Although "the majority" would 'argue' otherwise; the majority of doctors, and lawyers, are living their parents' dreams — not theirs.

(Under some of those 'white' coats; writers, artists, entrepreneurs, teachers, poets, strippers, marketers, and the like, are suffocated.)

The Power of the Human Mind

Consciousness is probably the 'sole' difference between a sleeping man and one that's awake. Owning to the fact that we experience the world in our very own minds. And, we use our minds to cause and/or to react to everything that happens "outside" our minds.

We are so used to, say, walking, that we forget that that first step that we took is the result of, say, the right leg, and, the right foot, effortlessly following what the mind has commanded them to do.

The mind is arguably the most powerful thing in the world.

I'm so foolishly convinced by that, that, to some extent, I'm of an opinion that a large number of people who die from incurable diseases are actually killed by the thought of knowing that they have such-and-such a disease — more than the 'terminal' disease itself.

The mind has the power to control body parts that we cannot voluntarily control. And, to test that, I used a friend as a 'guinea pig.'

I poured him some juice. I then watched as he emptied the glass.

After he took his last sip of what was left of his 2nd glass of orange juice ... I told him that I 'peed' in the juice that he just so enjoyed.

(I was pulling his leg, but nonetheless, he "bought" my story.)

... He looked at me. He rolled his eyes. He looked at the "empty" glass. He looked at me again. And then, he "rushed" to the loo ... Eighteen seconds or so later — I heard the poor soul "throw up."

Remember, I didn't touch him, or, put anything in the glass except orange juice. But these words, "I peed in your juice ..." — words that were then 'planted' in his mind, were powerful enough, after being entertained as a thought, to cause "whatever muscles" that contract when one vomits (muscles that we can't 'voluntarily' control) — to do their thing — and that 'ultimately' made him vomit.

... A few minutes later, just before I was about to be "slapped," I told him that I was joking. He survived, and, so did our friendship.

(Er, ... kids "Please do try this at home.")

To Be Schooled and Fooled

Like some cheesy back-to-school ads assert, "School is cool." But I have a love-and-hate relationship with school and being schooled.

School has the "potential" to be one of the most, if not the most, "powerful" institutions to humankind. But, regrettably, ... it is not.

The one thing that school does better than any other institution; is brainwashing students to blindly follow instructions. And as if that isn't enough; school teaches students to "conform." ... It all starts with the school uniform. Try wearing pink trousers to a blue-trousered-school-uniform school ... to be sent home is customary. That is punishment for he who fails (or refuses) to 'look like' other kids.

... School also bullies unique individuals to act, be, and, look alike. That's probably the reason behind the silly 'invention' of uniforms.

What's more, all that most subjects required was a good memory, as opposed to what we were "made" to believe — "intelligence."

This is basically how school works: Here is a Biology textbook; this is a head, that's a nose, that's a thigh, that's a spinal cord, that is an armpit, that is a shoulder, and, that is an ass. Butt, when you are around "grown-ups," use "buttocks," "behind," "backside," or, "rear end." Should you still wish to remain in the grown-ups' list of the *"Top Ten Well-Mannered Kids"* in the neighbourhood.

In an exam, if you recall all that is in the textbook, you will get full marks. The more "facts" you remember, the more marks you get.

The disturbing part is that even students who did not really understand what they worked so hard to 'memorize' still get to "pass." Well, ... that's provided that their "memory" does not "fail" them.

... All that one had to do was to read and then call to mind. Consume all known and proven facts; things based on the past, without questioning, or challenging, the known. Talk about parroting!

At times, she who is "educated" is nothing but somebody that is more instructed than the uneducated. The lucky uninstructed few.

Some artists fail grades merely because they had low math marks.

Agnes George de Mille, a "renowned" Choreographer, provoked thoughts when she "asserted" that, "A good education is usually 'harmful' to a dancer. A good calf is better than a good head."

With the exception of subjects like math, accounting, science, and other subjects which demanded one to understand a formula, for them to be able to "solve" a problem; all that one needed to be a "top student," was to "remember" more than one's classmates.

A student that 'gets' 5% in an exam — will still get to be a "Top student," so long as her "classmates" get 4% or less in the exam.

A good memory has for long been an illusional equivalent of intelligence. It's no wonder that most people who achieve wonders are either unschooled — or dropouts. For they don't worship convention, and, they refuse to entertain, and maintain, the status quo.

Both men who "contributed" immensely to the invention and the advancement of personal computers are 'dropouts.' One goes by the name of Steve Jobs — the other, ... by the name of Bill Gates.

"We don't have education, we have inspiration. If I was educated, I would be a damn fool."

— Bob Marley

Spend More on Books Than on Groceries

I have deliberately developed a "stupid" habit of spending a huge portion of the money 'reserved' for groceries, at bookshops. And, because of that peculiar habit; I either slept hungry or on a tummy full of nothing but brown bread, baked beans, and, black coffee.

A lot of people, people who think that they know better, say that that's a silly thing to do. But I always justify that both a full tummy and hunger are temporary. But the knowledge that I acquire isn't.

As a matter of fact, ... I have a lot to 'show' for all the books that I have read, say, three or so years back. However, I don't really have any 'notable' things (not even one) to show for last night's supper.

White People Can Dance

In this alluring world of ours, different people have different ways of "expressing" themselves. To dance too is to "express" oneself.

Therefore, if Tiego writes solely to express himself, then it matters not how "good" or "bad" his writings are. He is a writer. Because to do is to be a doer. And besides, both 'good' and 'bad' are subjective ... Furthermore, it is the dancing that makes dancing, dancing. And not, in a way, how "good" or "bad" the dancer dances.

(Allow me to 'lease' wisdom [via a proverb] from our Indian brothers and sisters, "To watch us dance is to hear our hearts speak.")

Stupid People
Are a Myth

A book populated with proven facts (the past) is handed to Zandi. She is forced to study its contents. An exam is written, and then, a test mark is given. She gets 8 percent, and, 'stupid' she is labelled.

In spite of that, ... I don't believe that there are "stupid" people.

I assert that the world just has artists who are required ~~and forced~~ to master science, and, scientists who are 'required' to master art.

(Chances are that your belittling words are "suffocating" the artist in the poor kid that you are constantly coercing 'accountancy' on.)

Things Were
Thoughts

I don't really know 'where' you are as you read this book. But one thing for sure is that; somewhere around you lie creations of man.

That "skyscraper" outside your window; whatever that was used to transport you from your home to your workplace; and the book which's *Page Nineteen* you are currently reading ... was, at some stage, ... nothing but "an idea" in the mind of some "dreamer."

(The difference between achievers + perpetual dreamers; is having courage, conquering the fear of failure, taking action, and, most importantly, having the 'wisdom' to ignore what other people had to "say" about one's dream, and, the odds of it being 'realizable.')

Black People Don't Swim, They Survive!

The fact that "Mandla" broke some woman's heart is not excuse enough for that woman to rule out every man that introduces himself as "Mandla," as a 'potential' other half. To hell with statistics!

While drowning and desperately fighting for my life: I watched Mr. Thompson, my then history teacher, watch me drown. He was the closest to me, with regards to proximity, but instead of him lending a hand ... he ordered other students to try to save me. Apparently, he was scared that he too would "drown." I found that strange ...

... Because someone once told me that "overweight" people defy gravity when in a swimming pool. Anyways, as soon as I was submerged, I did what I thought was a 'backstroke.' Little did I know that I was making my friends' effort to rescue me from the muddy water ... harder with every backstroke that I took. As I was moving further away from the spot in which I 'disappeared' into. Silly me!

To cut a slippery story short, Kabelo Masuku beat "everybody" to finding + rescuing me. Which shows that not all "heros" fight fire for a living. This one writes code to keep his landlord's lips zipped.

(The attitude of the 9th Jew that you'll meet tomorrow, won't necessarily be the same as that of the 8 Jews that you met yesterday.)

The Secret Behind Reading Books

Out of all the issues that I have discussed, questioned, and, ranted about, in this book — "not reading" — is by far the "saddest."

Sad to say, a lot of people hated school so much that they decided that their acquiring of 'knowledge' will end when they reach "the end of their studies." However, reading and studying are not one.

At the core of reading lies will. While 'studying' is merely an act of gathering, 'hopefully' understanding, memorizing, and, ultimately being "tested" on what one has memorized — by he who taught.

Take any "random" book. Whatever that is "written" in there ... is the wisdom (regarding whatever 'subject' that the book is about) that the author was 'kind enough' ... to share with those who are wise enough ... to invest their "time" ~~and/or money~~ in that book.

That then means that if you read, say, a marketing book, that was authored by someone with 40 years of 'experience' as a marketer; you're basically gaining wisdom that took the author four decades to acquire, in "a week," and, a hundred, or three hundred, pages.

I don't even want to mention the money that readers paid for that book; as the proportion of the money spent and the 'insights' that the readers have acquired, vary so much that the money spent on a book makes authors appear to be "taken for a ride" by readers.

Without reading, the most that your "knowledge base" will have, is what it already has. But in today's rapidly changing markets and industries; the "facts" that you were "fed in school" in Nineteen-Eighty-Nine ... could be of little — or no value — as you read this.

Since we are 'somewhat' what we think and what we know. How logical is one's ambition to be a more knowledgeable person, and, a "better thinker" ... when one and books are like 'oil and water'?

I truly looooooooooooooove and value reading books so much that I actually regard "a recommendation" of a goooood book as a gift.

(A library is to one's mind; what gym is to one's muscles. Question is ... what portion of your income goes to personal development?)

"Rich people have large libraries, poor people have large TV's."

– Dan Kennedy

Wisdumb of the Crowds

The large number of people uttering the "same" opinion does not necessarily make the opinion "superior" to that, with an opposing point of view, uttered by one person. Superiority isn't democratic.

... Maybe the 'collective' intellectual capability of 'every person' on earth "put together" ... would have not surpassed the exceptional intellectual capability that *Albert Einstein* was "blessed" with. Or else, that would mean that learners are smarter than their teacher.

(Simply put, a team made of 9 overweight kids will not necessarily run "faster" than the opposition made of 'one' underweight kid.)

The Need to Need to Need

Somebody is jobless. But he owes Nobody.

Somebody gets a job. Somebody then gets into 'debt' because of the new job. A new place just to be closer to work, a car to get to work on time, and a new wardrobe for him to look like other kids.

Somebody now "needs" the job to pay off the "debt."

But it is because of the job that Somebody got into debt. So, ... in essence, Somebody got a job to need a job.

Debt is slavery.

The Fear of Failure

We're brainwashed, from an early age, to avoid failure at all costs. A great deal of students who "fail a grade," more often than not, change schools ... as their fellow classmates' "mocking," in a way, makes them feel like failures, appear "stupid," or, at times, both.

Inevitably, most people settle for a "strategy" that sort of provides a refuge from failure; not doing. However, succeeding and not failing are not one. Granted, without doing one cannot fail. But one cannot succeed either. Also, even if one decides to settle for the refuge that not doing promises; one is still not immune to death.

... That there is what I always remind myself whenever doubt, fear, and procrastination, bend over backwards to conspire against me and whatever that I would like to actualize. Furthermore, in every single failure there is a valuable reward ... a lesson. To fail is merely to know of a path that "does not lead to" where you aspire to be.

Society really needs to adopt a habit of celebrating "failures." For their failures show courage. Something that the world is, and will forever be, "under the supply" of. And, what is scarce, is valuable.

(I say, the next time you fail; take yourself out. The courage shown and the 'lesson' acquired are worth celebrating, don't you think?)

The Power of Thoughts

Like I said earlier, we experience life within our minds. The thoughts, the feelings, the perceptions, the dreams, the memories, et cetera; all take place within our minds. That being so, the world is within us.

The mind is abstract, therefore, intangible. It is the brain that has a physical existence; not the mind. Just like how you can touch a pregnant woman's tummy, while you can't really touch pregnancy.

For that reason, nobody can really dictate what you can, or cannot, think about. Therefore, a prisoner whose thoughts are limited to nothing and nowhere, but prison — is serving twice the sentence.

We are all in control of our fate. And that is not because we have the privilege of choosing what happens to us. It is merely because of the fact that we are blessed with the privilege of choosing how to look at, and how we react to, every thing that happens to us.

A man who has just been given the boot can either worry about where and how is he going to get the money to pay for his bills — or he can "celebrate" the thought of not having an employment contract — a piece of paper that dictates where he spends eight-hours (add to that the time spent commuting) of his weekdays.

Man is mostly limited by his own mind. Almost all the actions that he does not take are dictated by what he 'believes' to be his limit.

At the core of people's excuses for not doing, shipping, publish-ing, or launching, lies fear. But fear is nothing but a state of mind. Which means that it is in one's control. What's worse is that being fearful rarely avoids, or betters, whatever that one is so fearful of.

We are today what we thought yesterday. And, we will be what we will be "tomorrow," because of what we are thinking today.

The most important thing to take from my 'silly' done-without-a-white-coat-orange-juice-experiment; is that the human mind be-lieves every single thing that we feed it. Whether it is true or not.

So, in a nutshell, the mind cannot differentiate what is true from what is imagined. Hence, the mind 'believes' whatever we feed it.

I think that 'wet dreams' are an epitome that supports that claim. The mind 'believes' that sex is being had, as a result, an orgasm is.

(We don't really have control over a lot of thoughts that occasionally occupy our mind; especially the 'negative' ones — but we can choose which thoughts to entertain and which ones to get rid of.)

The Difference Between a Woman and a Girl

A woman 'encourages' her man to actualize his dreams — while a girl religiously 'competes' with her man's dreams for his attention.

The same applies: when differentiating between a man and a boy.

When one thinks of their lover; one should be overwhelmed by the successes that their partner's presence 'helped' them achieve; not by the dreams that one had to let go; just to appear considerate.

(Behind every successful half, there is a not-so nagging other half.)

I Hate Green Skinny Jeans and Leather Pants

... I honestly do. But, I truly loooooooooooooooooooove how those who wear them do not 'give a damn' about what Mokokoma and 'the rest of the world' thinks about them — their fashion taste — and the clothes that they so love, and, feel comfortable in. Salute!

Consumer Involvement Yields Profits

In the olden days, factory owners used to make things. They then spent millions of dollars on making adverts that yelled at, mostly, irrelevant people. People whose take mattered not to such owners.

Today, entrepreneurs who are courageous enough to involve their patrons in all possible aspects of their 'product development' have a forever quite landlord to show for the fruits of such a valiant act.

Imagine the excitement of a reader, after she sees that the author changed the initial title of a chapter as per her suggestion; or the joy of a reader that finds out, during an unplanned visit to a bookstore, that the author went with the book cover that she vote for.

Let me not even start with the number of the people who'll get to know about the book; as a result of the reader's infinite bragging escapades. That alone is enough to help a publisher that overestimated the value that a book will add to its readers, "break-even."

Time Waits for Norman

A minute is nothing but a reference to the duration of a particular moment. Meaning that time was, time is, and time will forever be.

It is the moments that disappears and passes us by. Not time. We are only able to live and experience moments. Not time. Therefore, time cannot be spent. Moreover, a "waste of time" is subjective.

Sleeping, or watching TV, could be "the most productive" thing that the man doing it, could be doing, under his circumstances.

"It Pays the Bills" The Motto of Modern Slaves

Do you wake up "very early" in the a.m. to go to a job that you hate? Are you tolerating your job solely because "it pays the bills"?

How much of "the bills" were brought to being by your job?

A job that you so desperately 'need' for you to be able to pay the bills; while it is the job that brought nearly all the bills to being.

The rent for the new place that you moved into; just to be closer to work. The car that you made a five-year financial commitment to; just so you get to work on time. The clothes that you bought on credit; just so you too look "presentable" like "other kids."

Do you work terribly hard, every weekday, for a month. Get paid. Pay the bills. Be terribly broke. And then wait for payday. Rinse and repeat. Until death will eventually do your lifeless life a favour?

If that is the case, then you are a modern slave; tied down, not by chain, but by a paycheck; and an illusional sense of "job security."

If "settling" for an average income, average achievements, and, a "secure job," is a sign of maturity — like we were programmed to believe — then being "matured" is "too childish" for my liking.

The only thing that we're running out of, that is worth trying hard to utilize, is ~~time~~ moments. Since no one really knows how many sunrises, and sunsets, are left for him or her to witness — before there is a six-meter divide of soil — between them, and, the living.

"A worker is a part-time slave. The boss says when to show up, when to leave, and what to do in the meantime. He is free to carry his control to humiliating extremes, regulating, if he feels like it, the clothes you wear."

— Bob Black

The Receipt Doesn't Make
the Product

Formal education is not "that" important. It is the "education" in "formal education" — that is important. That is what matters.

Education is merely the process whereby school and its employees feed students with 'systematic' instruction. Education is a body of language that one acquires while being "educated" or schooled.

The most important thing is the teachings — not the teachers, not how much the "school fees" costs, and definitely, not the school.

When a bakery is looking for a baker ... shouldn't priority be given to the job seekers' baking skills; as opposed to "where" they were taught how to preheat an oven, and, how to mix flour with eggs?

Does the 'manner' in which one acquires a laptop affect what the laptop is? Would it be less of a laptop, should it have been stolen? Will that affect, say, the laptop's processing speed? I think so, not.

"Education" is important, very. It is 'where and how' one acquires the knowledge that I find irrelevant. What matters is that I answer "two," when I am asked what one plus one is; not "where" I was taught that — who taught me that — or how I was taught that.

I think we are hopelessly blinded by a tiny illusion. An eleven-letter word that is subtly sold by educational institutions — "credibility."

Granted, I too would not trust a self-taught doctor to operate me. For I am also blinded by credibility. But that does not change what the self-taught doctor is capable of doing. A "self-taught" person too is an educated being. Whether we acknowledge them or not.

(Besides, not every remarkable person is educated, and, not every "educated" person is remarkable — most are merely "not bad.")

A Winner of an Argument is a Loser of Time

People say "things." Opposing opinions gets shared. Opinions are forced on others. And, inevitably, arguments are brought to being.

Ideally, this is how an "argument" that I partake in should happen. I share my points of view on the subject matter with Someone; I then listen to Someone's standpoint. And then, we both shut up.

For an argument does not really "have to" produce a "winner."

I don't really get into an argument to win. Seeing that arguments are, more often than not, based on nothing but subjectivity. And, subjective arguments rarely produce a "gold medalist." As each contestant will also double as the judge.

Besides, what will I really be winning, when all that I manage to do is to get someone to see whatever that we are arguing about, the same way as I see it? What exactly does a Christian that manages to convert an atheist into a Christian win? Eternal life?

I too have been "challenged." On- and offline. But I always share my opinion, listen to theirs, and, I then tell the other person that I think that they're right. Even when I am still of an opposing stand. Their ego gets fed, and, I get 'more time' to do work that matters.

The other thing is that, ... when a person is "proven wrong" in an argument, esp. an argument that had "spectators," their ego gets bruised — and at times — their intelligence gets questioned. And, as a result, most people will stick to their initial opinion or stand. Even after they have realized that your rationalization makes more sense than theirs. To get a person to concede is thorny.

(The best way to "win" an argument is to avoid one. Seeing that for one to "win" an argument; one must be willing to lose time.)

The Primary Goals of Different Social Classes

In his book, *The Top 10 Distinctions Between Millionaires, and, the Middle Class*, Keith C. Smith asserts that, "The primary goal of the very poor is survival. The primary goal of the middle-class is comfort. While the primary goal of the very rich is freedom."

Most people are likely to argue that the poor and the middle class are also free. Well, there is nothing surprising with such an assertion. I think that that will depend on what is meant by "freedom."

But waking up to a job that one hates; a job that one is forced to tolerate solely cuz it pays the bills; is nothing but modern slavery.

(Until man is at a point where he doesn't have to trade his time to make a living; he is not really free. He is merely a part-time slave.)

The Definition of Achievement

The *New Oxford American Dictionary*, native to Apple's OS, put in to words, "Achievement" as "... a thing done successfully."

But I think that is a bit "boring." Here is my own little definition:

An achievement is -- an expression, and exhibition, of how fearful, or courageous, one has been. And, also, at the core of a person's achievements — one will either find fear, or courage, not "luck."

Local Sucks to the Locals

An American artist that is scheduled to perform in South Africa is, more often than not, likely to sell more tickets than a South African artist that is scheduled to perform in South Africa.

It is either because of the fact that locals believe that anything international is superior, or, it is simply scarcity being itself. Valuable.

Anything that's easy to get (procedure or price) is perceived as less valuable. Guys from out-of-town easily sweep women in so-and-so towns off their feet. Merely because they're "new in town." And, without fail, though it only lasts for a week or six, new-kids-in-the-block* always seem to rock, or, they at least appear to do so.

(*That excludes weirdos. They are found "boring" from day one.)

Abundance is Overrated

I was once depressed because I didn't have a book to read. But, a week after that, I found myself stressed, because I couldn't decide which of the 'twelve' books, that I have just bought, to start with.

I have over 11,450 songs in my iTunes library. But I "do not" listen to even a tenth of them. Some I have never listened to. And, I am unlikely to have the time, or the desire, to listen to most of them.

(Generally, people need less than a quarter of what they "want.")

Wealth is a By-Product, Not a Goal

Spike Lee, Mark Shuttleworth, Bill Gates, Steve Jobs, Madam C. J. Walker, Sergey Brin, Oprah Winfrey, and other geniuses who have achieved a great deal of wealth, were not really "chasing money."

They had 'purposes' which they believe they were born to contribute to humanity. Passions that they were wise enough to pursue.

All the financial rewards are by-products of their "real" successes.

Steve Jobs is widely quoted saying that, "Being the richest man in the cemetery doesn't matter to me... Going to bed at night saying we have done something wonderful. That is what matters to me."

Being Great is a Sacrifice

At the core of being a great creator lies producing above average creations. And that, unavoidably, ... intimidates "average" people.

To be a great writer whose writings are 'intellectually' demanding; one must be willing to let go of the "not-so-intellectual" readers.

Scores of 'first-rate' artists produce 'third-rate' art because of their desperate, and unfruitful, efforts to appeal to every single person.

(However, trying to please everybody is a waste of time. For there are countless boring people who find 'interesting' people boring.)

"You cannot be both fashionable
and first-rate."

— Logan Pearsall Smith

Rely on Nobody but Yourself

To get things done; learn to rely on nobody but yourself.

When collaborating, you should let other reliable people's reliableness be a plus. Not a deal maker, or, a deal breaker. Some people will take you for a ride. While life will happen to the few honest people who 'wanted' to stick to 'their word' by playing their part.

(The good thing about relying on oneself is that one knows exactly where to find one's self. Should one find oneself stood up by self.)

What Makes a Great Headline?

What makes a headline that asks a question so powerful?

The answer lies in the fact that when a writer asks a question; it forces the reader to think of possible answers to the question. It instills curiosity in the reader, and, furthermore, people hate not knowing; so they'll do what is necessary to appease their curiosity.

It goes without saying, the headline will mostly appeal to readers with an interest in whatever subject that the question is based on.

For example, "What makes a great headline ... a great headline?," will, more often than not, solely appeal to readers who also write.

But should I have had, "Questions make a good headline," as a headline, this writing would have probably attracted fewer readers. Seeing that that headline would have "summed up" this writing.

Creatives Are Underpaid

Ideas are the most valuable assets in the world. Inevitably, people who come up with great ideas 'usually' end up with great wealth.

That 'bakery' down the road sells biscuits. The shop opposite the bakery sells clothes. And the shop next to the bakery sells computers. That's their "offerings" — tangible "manufactured" products.

However, creatives' products are ideas, and, they are intangible.

Because the generation of ideas does not require a considerable amount of "raw materials," countless creatives let the harsh reality that they are paid far way less than what they are worth slide.

For their "products" to be brought to being; a bakery must spend money on flour, sugar, milk, etc. All that creatives "spend" is time.

The advertising industry is an epitome of remarkable thinkers tied down by minuscule paychecks. Most settle for the "glamorous" lifestyle that the industry promises — as a consolation prize.

One remarkable idea alone is enough to secure an agency a client that will bring in millions of dollars in annual billings. But the salaries of the agencies' "gooses-that-lay-golden-eggs" are disturbing.

Throughout the course of their careers, ... creatives come up with ideas that make their employers billions; which then helps them in building wealth and achieving financial freedom for their families. Yet, ... most creatives retire with a disturbingly 'dull' bank balance.

And, at times, I can't help but feel that the monthly salary paid to most creatives, should have actually been the creatives' daily rate.

... Oh well, I guess the wealth "deservedly" goes to those who are courageous enough to delay gratification ... while taking the hard work, and the "uncertainties" of, creating employment for others.

(The "Fat cats" take almost all the profits. Not because they have worked the hardest — but because they take almost all the risks.)

Why Most Relationships Don't Last

I don't think that I make a good boyfriend. I just make a 'killer' ex.

(Anyhow, ... I am still going to share my two cents' worth below.)

Boy meets girl. ~~There's lust at first sight.~~ Boy likes girl. And, should girl like boy too; it is inevitable that girl will "play" girl that girl assumes boy seeks. Even if that means girl being girl that girl is not.

But when boy and girl start out as people in each other's lives; be it as friends, neighbours, colleagues, or acquaintances; they get to know the real other. Hence I think that relationships are more likely to last when they just 'happen' — as opposed to being proposed.

When a guy is around a girl that he likes; she will play the girl that she thinks that the guy wants. Should she like him too. But that is not really "getting to know" someone. That is called acting. Chris Rock quipped that, "When you meet Somebody for the first time, you are not meeting them. You are meeting their representative."

(*Disclaimer:* Ahem, ... I "guarantee" not, a successful "romantic" relationship, with any of your colleagues, neighbours, or, friends.)

Poor Design ≠ Bankruptcy

Ineffectual design is one of life's greatest tragedies. Add to that, entrepreneurs who opt for a cheap better-than-nothing type of a designer; while they afford the expertise of a remarkable designer.

Without doubt, a business will still get to make money, even when its corporate identity or product packaging is of third-rate design. But such a business's bottom-line could have easily been doubled, if not quadrupled, by simply having invested in a first-rate designer.

On account of second-rate design: Countless websites lose browsers that could've browsed for a few minutes longer. And, having had a red-coloured link — as opposed to the less contrasting grey that the "affordable" designer chose — could have increased the odds of a browser sending that enquiry email, making that phone call, or, buying whatever it is that the website was created to sell.

And, in other cases, because of inferior design: A business is perceived as cheap, and as a result, they appear unprofessional. Attention that could have been perpetuated is lost. Prospects leave the website before reading the most important part of the web page.

A company that claims to be "professional," while, say, its corporate identity looks "cheap," and shoddy; is comparable to an overweight sales consultant that sells gym memberships for a living.

Professional design is like exercising. While not exercising will definitely not kill one; exercising will, without a doubt, improve one's quality of life. In innumerable cases, more often than not, all that companies with, say, a $1,000,000 turnover need — is to invest $10,000 in design — for them to realize a $10,000,000 turnover.

All that that will require — is the expertise, insights, and wisdom, of a remarkable designer. Be she a user-interface, user experience, graphic, interior, packaging, or, product designer. Granted, ... she will not come cheap. But the proportion of what she charges, and what the entrepreneur will reap, makes her a worthy investment.

So, in a nutshell, the lowest returns that an entrepreneur is willing to settle for; is not necessarily the optimum profits that that entrepreneur can realize. The "most possible" returns that she can squeeze out of the investments that she has made is.

Case Study: Dithapelo Kgonyane, a friend of mine, once lent me a book that seemed like a great read. But because of the book designer's poor choice of typography; I tried to read it, not once, but three times. In all attempts, ... I couldn't read further than a page.

An undersized font too is deadly; but it is nothing compared to a font that is illegible, or hard to read, even when it is oversized.

In all attempts, I had to squint; and that strained my eyes. So I had to stop reading. Because of the headache that the squinting bred.

Granted, this seems like a minuscule incident. But that bad choice of typography lessened the book's chances of "going viral." So, whether the author's aim was to spread ideas, or, to make money — either way, the designer dramatically reduced his chances of realizing whatever returns that he aspired to achieve with the book.

I would have read the book, and then bought myself a copy (just to keep as a souvenir), even though I would have read his. And, more importantly, I was likely to recommend the book to friends whom I knew would find value in reading the book. That one recommendation alone would've had the potential to lead to hundreds, if not thousands, purchases of copies of that book. And that could've easily been achievable in less than a year of that one recommendation.

The book's author might be satisfied with whatever number of copies that he managed to sell; but he could've definitely sold more.

This is an illustration of how 'small' things such as poor choice of typography affect how far ideas, knowledge, insights and wisdom spread. A first-rate product is easily killed by second-rate design.

The Best Thing to Talk to John About

The best person, subject, or thing, to talk to John about, is John.

People are forever thinking of themselves, their needs, their problems, their wants, and, their dreams. John's headache is of more importance to him than the famine that is killing people in Ghana.

The only time that you can talk about yourself, or your product, is only when you, or your product, will help John solve <u>his</u> problems.

So, when selling, say, condoms, to him; don't waste your time telling him about your company's history or philosophy; how passionate you are in preventing unwanted pregnancies; or how durable the latex that your company uses is — sell him a "peace of mind."

Don't sell him the features of your gym's treadmill; sell him the fit, healthy, sexually appealing, and, hard-to-resist he that he will be.

(Likewise, don't sell him your history. Sell him his potential future.)

As Un-prioritizing As ... ? A Rapper!

Do you first realize your need to go "somewhere." And then get a car or a taxi to take you "somewhere?" Or, do you, after realizing that a car or a taxi can take you "somewhere," go "somewhere"?

There needs to be a function to be realized; for form to justify its existence. Therefore, form should always be 'dictated' by function.

There first has to be a message to be expressed; before a rhyme is written. The art lies in the artist's artistry to express something meaningful — using rhymes — not in the artist's ability to squeeze some sense out of an already written "nonsensical" rhyme.

Homemade Meals Are Overrated

Not all meals that are made at home are healthy. Not all healthy meals were made at home. "Homemade" and healthy aren't one.

Over and above that, it takes time, electricity, and, innumerable different ingredients, to make even the simplest meal of them all. So, "takeouts" aren't as "expensive" as they're painted out to be.

Furthermore, the thought of taking two hours to cook a meal that one will devour in seven minutes; sounds too absurd for my liking.

(But with that said, cooking is one of the best way to "unwind.")

Repetition: A Tax Paid for Having an Unremarkable Idea

Even in the course of our times cluttered with countless marketing messages; a remarkable idea only needs to be heard or seen once; for it to be tattooed in the minds of those that it is exposed to.

Advertising, by and large, relies on repetition for the advertised to stand a chance of being thought of, and hopefully, being bought.

With enough repetitions; even a song that you hate will stick in your mind. And, sooner or later, you might even find yourself humming a song that you passionately hate, or, find so irritating.

While the few entrepreneurs that have "first-rate" ideas are busy reaping profits; those with 'second-rate' ideas are busy repeating.

"Advertising is the tax you pay for being unremarkable."
— Robert Stephens

(I doubt that a woman that has successfully managed to sweep a man of his feet; would have to introduce herself more than once.)

Not All Eggs Will Hatch

Never make plans with money that is "owed" to you. Even when whoever that owes you 'acknowledges' that he indeed owes you.

Some people will take chances. While life will "happen" to those few people who genuinely wanted to pay you what is due to you.

The only money that you have; is the only money that you have.

That is to say, some eggs do hatch on time; some eggs hatch later than expected or agreed on; while some eggs will sort of miscarry.

(In a nutshell, a debtor's admission of a debt won't help the creditor put food on the table, or pay rent, until the debt is settled.)

"You can complain because roses
have thorns, or you can
rejoice because thorns have roses."

— Tom Wilson

The Lifespan of Gratitude

He longs for something. He gets the thing. He is then grateful. He gets used to having the thing. Eventually, he becomes ungrateful.

Find a starving man. Give him baked beans, bread, and water. He will, without a doubt, be grateful. Do that every single day, three times a day, for a month or nine. Before you know it, he will start ranting and raving about how much he has had enough of baked beans, bread, and water. Forgetting that before you started giving him the little that you could; he went for days without eating.

Find an unemployed woman. Promise her a thousand dollar salary. She will momentarily feel blessed. Allow a few months and paydays to pass. And, she will soon rant to those who care enough to lend an ear; about how "used," underpaid, and, taken for a ride she is.

Similarly, material possessions will never bring one everlasting contentment. A man dreams of retiring the pedestrian in him. He gets blessed with a car; a few installments later, he wants a faster car.

A woman born into an extremely poor family, sweeps an extremely wealthy man off his feet. She gets married to the "poor" wealthy man. She then moves from moving around by a bicycle to driving a Ferrari. In the twinkling of an eye; she gets used to the possessions — and having such deep pockets — and grateful she no longer is.

And, all of a sudden, having a lot of money seems "normal" to her; and the next thing you know — she cheats with a penniless man.

Come to think of it, generally speaking, women with well-to-do other halves commit adultery with men with shallower pockets.

Find a person that has no legs. Give him two legs so he too can walk. He will, without doubt, be grateful. But, sooner or later, he will start complaining about him having "funny" toes, feet that are too small, or too big, or the fact that he has no shoes to wear.

Even with the problems that you have; the little that you own; and the "rough patches" that you're going through — there are gazillions of people out there, who would feel blessed to at least be in your shoes. While you are busy complaining that you have an ugly handwriting; there are people who would kill to have at least one hand. Likewise, there are 'dead people' who would kill to be alive.

(Er, ... when was the last time that you were thankful for seeing a new day, being able to walk, or, having a family that loves you?)

Somebody is a Former Nobody

There is always a Nobody blended in our surroundings; a Nobody whose deeds, and genius, will soon be celebrated by everybody.

That Somebody that you are so touched and inspired by; might actually be the Nobody that you failed to "notice," a few weeks back; solely because their hustling wasn't paying dividends as yet.

There was a time when Nelson Mandela was, nothing but, just another human being, to South Africans and the rest of the world.

That 'street kid' begging on that street corner, might later be the president that will demand an increase of the social grant for the elderly. Something that will be of great benefit to the quality of your life, in a few decades' time, when you're a then senior citizen.

(A "Somebody" is a person that achieved so much that the world had no choice but to promote her from a Nobody to a Somebody.)

The Idiot Box: Who's Fooling Who?

Apart from the opportunity to have something to "gossip" about; what value did the last episode of *"The Bold & Beautiful,"* something that demanded thirty-minutes of your time, add to your life?

It has been just over a year since I decided to give my TV away.

Just before I gave it away, my mother said that I must have lost my mind. And, that was not because I was about to give the idiot box away; I was giving it to her after all. But because my mother believed that I will not have anything to "refresh" my mind with.

But I told her that I either read a book, or go to gym, for that.

She still thought that I was bananas! I don't know about you; but I don't really have anything to show for my twenty or so years of watching TV. That is why I decided to get rid of the TV that I had.

This is basically how television works:

Channel so-and-so buys television programs which they think will be able to get the masses glued to the idiot box, all day, everyday.

Channel so-and-so then gets advertisers to sell the masses something. The more people that Channel so-and-so is able to entice; the more money the channel will make from its advertising spaces.

The channel then dedicates almost a third of what the masses believe to be a 30-minute episode — to "selling" them something.

The thing that I hate about dramas that do not occur in seasons; is that they take "forever" to tell you what they could tell you in one episode. Actually, most producers "stretch" the story line on purpose; just so they don't run out of something to say. For their bread-and-butter depends on their "beating around the bush."

On the contrary, a movie has, say, an hour or two, to illustrate the point that it was made to convey. And, though, some try to make some extra money through product placements; no advert will interrupt you while you are busy being entertained and/or educated.

It is said that an average American watches over 35 hours of TV a week. That is over 1820 hours in one year. I used to average two hours of watching TV per day. *Two hours* x *365 days* is equals to 730 hours in a year. That is way more than enough time. For one to build an empire, or, to even, change the world. Should one be blessed with a good supply of ambition, guts, and, perseverance.

Let me put that into an employee / employer / work context. Two hours of watching TV a day is equivalent to over 4 months of an 8-hour day's work. And that "includes" an hour long lunch break!

There is nothing wrong with the idiot box. It is just that I find that there is always something more productive that I could do; instead of drooling over women with flawless skin, fake hair, and, enough make up to 'bury' the script they were hired to bring to life under.

Groucho Marx quipped that, "I find television very educating. Every time somebody turns on the set, I go into the other room and read a book." My other favourite remark on television is by Noël Coward; and he said that "TV is for appearing on. Not for looking at."

A Minimalist is an Enduring Conqueror of Complexity

There is a confession that I publicly display on my graphic design journal. And, it reads, *"hello. I'm a designer + simplicity addict."*

Sad to say, there are two "disadvantages" to being a minimalist.

Firstly, it is very taxing to achieve such a state, without blurring the message that the design is intended to convey — or without interfering with the functionality that the design is meant to carry out.

Secondly, the rest of the world will judge both your work and your worth, solely based on how "simple" the end product is. In most cases such people will be of an opinion that you were "overpaid."

Nonetheless, it is not how easy it is to replicate what a minimalist has created, that makes them "expensive." It is the wisdom of knowing which visual elements to cut down and which ones to leave out, that makes a minimalist unparalleled, hence, expensive.

"Simplicity" is not a state that is limited to form. Function too has its own complexities — by that very fact — simplicity is practicable.

The steps and the clicks that a website browser is required to survive before she can place an order on an online store too can, in almost all instances, be made simpler than they already are.

An automatic automobile is an excellent example. While a manual car is relatively 'easy' to drive; an automatic car is 'easier' to drive.

(If the way in which something looks, or, the manner in which it works, can be simplified; I assert that its creator's job is not done.)

Investors Rarely Change the World

Generally, an investor is merely someone who tries to get as many dollars as she possibly can; out of every dollar that she invests in a dream, a dreamer, a project, an employee, or, a business.

But it's the dreamer that changes the world. Not the bed provider.

The closest that an investor will get to changing the world; is by financing a dreamer. And, that is if, and only if, the investor is sold that the dreamer's dream will yield financial returns.

A million dollars is exactly that; a million dollars — whether it was won, borrowed, or, stolen. But ideas are not "that" transposable.

It is those that come up with ideas and/or dreams that change the world; not their investors' deep pockets. Investors merely sponsor, say, writers, that have great stories to write, with a pen and paper.

Google's investors are replaceable, with ease. But Google isn't.

(The paper that William Shakespeare's work is written, or, printed on — is replaceable — but his work isn't — not by a long shot.)

The Irony of Thoughtful Friends

Friends are beautiful creatures; I think that they are a blessing.

Our friends usually have our best interest at heart. But, sad to say, our friends judge our limitations based own their own limitations.

My employer and I have been one since forever; and I too was not immune to being broke. I was broke ... when I got the phone call.

A loving, caring, and, thoughtful friend, gave me a call to tell me about some job opening. They needed a graphic designer. And he "knew" the person that has the final say as to who is to be hired.

He told me that, " ... this job pays this-and-that much a month!"

He probably said, "… this job pays this-and-that much a month!," about twenty times throughout the twenty-minute call.

You're probably thinking, "Wow! ... Some people have supportive friends." But if my friend really believed in the dream that I was working so hard to realize, like he pretends to be, why did he lure and distract the poor dreamer in me with an employment offer?

Isn't it ironic and hypocritical for a priest that claims to be protected by "the Almighty," to walk around town in a bullet proof vest?

(In a word, if you truly believe that someone can fly, like he does. Before he "attempts" to fly; get him a compass. Not a bandage.)

When I see a Stranger

I really don't know why. But when I see a kid; I try to envisage the man that he will be. And when I see a man; I imagine the boy that he was. And at times, I wonder if the boy in the man would have found life worth living; should he have known that he would end up with the man that he is. Women and girls aren't an exception.

Overweight People Underrate Working Out

Some people go to gym just to have a chiseled physique. There is nothing wrong with that. Looking good isn't such a "bad thing."

However, I go to gym to feel good, and more importantly, to fight yet another battle with the little voice at the back of my head. The little voice that always tell you than you can't, or, that you are too tired to continue. That little voice at the back of one's head limits zillions of unknowing people. And its limiting isn't limited to gym.

Innumerable artists are stuck with their 'secure' jobs. They turn a blind eye to their dream; while they're busy helping someone else realize his dream. Mostly because of the voice that reminds them of bills that need to be paid and the chance of their art not selling.

Although it's an ongoing battle; learning to quieten the little voice at the back of your head will help you to dramatically lessen, if not eliminate, the chances of you quitting; whenever the going gets tough. And, it goes without saying, we all have times where giving up seems like a safer, logical, and, "matured" thing to do.

The louder the voice is, and, the less successful that you are in not paying attention to the voice — the less you will achieve.

If a person is not occasionally enticed by the thought of giving up on their dream; it is either that person is dreaming what has already been dreamt before, or that person is not dreaming at all.

The aforementioned is just the 'psychological benefits' of working out. There are also numerous health benefits. Working out also increases endorphins, the body's "feel good" chemicals, which gives one a mood boost. Or, as some people called it, a "runner's high."

Working out is for me, by far, the best antidote for stress. And like we all know, the only people who are 'immune' to stress are dead.

Now enter my last attempt to get you on a treadmill:

Also, a good session of working out also does wonders to one's sex drive. And it usually helps men with erectile dysfunction, caused by poor blood flow to the genital region, to "get their act together."

(I have heard that sex sells. So, I hope that with my mentioning of sex drives and erections; you bought the worthiness of exercising.)

"Those who think they have not time
for bodily exercise will sooner
or later have to find time for illness."

— Edward Stanley

Wherever a Thinker is, is the Office

Offices aren't as important as they used to be a few decades back. Back then..., factories were what most workers had as their office.

But today, the world and its economies generously rewards those with the biggest intellectual, and, creative muscles. As opposed to the physical strength that factories demanded and rewarded. That being so, women and skinny men need to shut and start thinking.

An idea, a laptop, and, an Internet connection, is enough for one to build an empire, spread ideas, or, to make a difference in other people's lives. As a creative entrepreneur, the most important thing to my businesses is my mind — or rather, the ideas that my mind conceives. Everything else is of a lesser importance. That being so, never ask for directions to a thinker's office. Ask her where is she.

It Only Takes a Few Hundreds to Be a CEO

Owning a business is easy, and, it is not really an "achievement," like most people act, think, or, hint. All it takes is a few hundreds.

The truth is that anybody can be a CEO. Provided that they have a few hundreds and a week or two to register a company. And then will they be free to title themselves as a "Chief Executive Officer."

But, it's not one's position that matters; the question is, what's the turnover of the company that one is "Chief Executive Officering"?

If "Luck" Exists, then "Luck" is Man-made

Whiners have a terribly foolish habit of calling winners "lucky."

But behind every so-called "lucky" person, there is — hard work, not giving up, giving up things that are worth a hundred today for things that will be worth a million tomorrow, sleepless nights, the art of delaying one's gratification, and, last but not least, giving up being comfortable on Monday ... for a more comfortable Sunday.

The next time someone says that they are unlucky; ask them what have they sacrificed for them to be, or to have, what they believe they need to be, or to have, before they declare themselves lucky.

(Generally, people compare themselves with others based on what others are reaping. But rarely on the hard labour of their sowing.)

Why There'll Always Be More Undertakers Than Corpses

A job title that is made of a 'verb' that is followed by a "-er" suffix, does not really require "schooling." Whether we like it or not, regardless of one's education, or, competency: he who sings is a singer; he who writes is a writer; and he who designs is a designer.

The same applies with disc jockeys. Anybody with a Pentium II PC, a subwoofer, a CD or nine and no talent, can call themselves a DJ.

(He who does is a doer; irrespective of how 'terrible' the done is.)

Entertainment Isn't That Entertaining

Before you watch TV, be sure that you are done with your day's work; for you are about to watch other people do their work.

When you're at a stadium to 'watch' twenty grown-ups in shorts, chase one ball; be sure that your day's work is done. How silly would it be for you not to be able to do your work; simply because you went to some "office park" to watch other people do their work?

Entertainment is there to help one unwind, and, to take a break from work. Not to "compete" with one's work for one's attention.

Bear in mind that while you are busy watching some man kiss another man's woman; the two are busy making money, while you are watching them fake reality — or at times — fictionalize reality.

Books Shouldn't Be Written to Be Remembered

A great book betters a reader's thinking, more than it populates their mind with facts and dates. Such books add value to the remaining number of days that the reader is left with.

Instead of a book feeding me the date, and the name, of the first person to go to the moon; something that will still be the same in a hundred years' time; I would rather read a book that teaches me how to count. For there is life after reading a book, and, life is likely to 'demand' the counting skills that I would have then acquired.

So, I would rather fill your head with principles that you can apply to your life tomorrow; instead of overpopulating it with what happened yesterday. I mean, ... what will you do with your knowledge of who "the first man" to go to the moon was? ... Go to the sun?

So long as you can take at least one thing out of this book. Anything that will add value to what's left of your life. You don't even need to remember my name or the title of this book. All a student needs to remember is the teachings that the teacher taught; not the teacher. I don't even remember who taught me the alphabets.

SpongeBob™ > The News

I have replaced "the news" with cartoons. Merely because unlike with the news, cartoons rarely depress those who consume them.

Like I said, news providers will almost always only feed you negative stories. Because positivity doesn't sell. What is more, the word "impossible" does not really exist in the world of cartoons. Bingo!

(With cartoons I get two of the most powerful things that one can get from something. A good laugh, and, an attitude of possibility.)

Big Dreams are Funny

The bigger the dream; the funnier it is. Big dreams are to people who dream small; what a joke is to people with a sense of humor.

(I told a very close friend about my aspirations to write this book. And he laughed at me. Twice ... in three-minutes. I felt honoured.)

"Normal is getting dressed in clothes that you buy for work, and driving through traffic in a car that you are still paying for. In order to get to the job you need to pay for the clothes and the car, and the house you leave vacant all day so you can afford to live in it."

— Ellen Goodman

The "First Blacks" Are Overrated

To be the first person to moonwalk is, without doubt, an achievement. It is definitely a deed worth celebrating. And perhaps also noble enough to be penned and recorded in the books of history.

What makes celebrating "The first person to ..." sensible; is that before them, no other human being was able to do or to be this-or-that. Seeing that such achievements are mostly of things which were once regarded as "impossible" for a man to do, or, to be.

But is it really necessary for the world to honour "The first black" people to do something? What does that say about black people?

Unless, and only if, "The first black president" is celebrated solely as an indication of "transformation," celebrating "The first black president ..." is an insult to black people's leadership capabilities.

We're all equal in terms of our physical and intellectual capabilities. So, ... when someone who happens to be "white" achieves something; let us all celebrate the power that "human beings" possess.

And, when a 'black person' later does, or becomes, the very same thing that a 'white person' has done, or, become. Let him and his loved ones celebrate him being the second, third, fifth, or, the one hundred-and-thirtieth human being to find what has been found; do what has been done, or, to conquer what's already conquered.

Lebogang Nkoane once questioned, "... Why do we celebrate black achievements? We should be celebrating 'human' achievements."

Briefly, it is the never-done-before deeds that matters, and, that is worthy of our attention and salute. Not the 1st doer's skin colour.

(Er, ... I hope that I'm "the first black" to write such about blacks.)

A Rich Man's Work is a Poor Man's Gossip

One wealthy man "creates" a TV drama. He then hires a team of middle-class people to bring it to being. Once the drama goes live, millions and millions of poor and middle-class people watch it — and they then spend most of their time 'talking about' the drama.

"Oh, ... did you see the pink boots that Brooke wore last night?"

Alas, that's while the creator of the drama is either working, reading, sleeping, writing another drama, having sex, spending quality time with his family, or, reaping the fruits of ~~his~~ their hard labour.

A rich man hires a poor man. Though the poor makes the rich millions a month; he's paid a few thousands a month. As if that's not enough: when not making the rich richer; the poor spend most of their time telling others about things that the rich do, say, or own.

While countless people are busy 'talking' about the iPhone; Steve Jobs and Apple's shareholders are either busy counting the money that they made from the fourth generation of the iPhone, or, they are busy "working hard" at bringing the fifth generation to being.

Generally, people who make billions from 'TV dramas' do not even have a television set at home. Talk about an extremely healthy person that owns a McDonalds franchise, or, a non-smoking salesman that is making millions of dollars, a month, from selling cigarettes!

While you are taking your precious time, time that you could have used to make art, to talk about some artist's art — who is talking about you, or, your art? And, what progress does your art realize?

(Taking an hour to "talk about" how someone else makes twenty-four thousand dollars a day, is a foolish way to 'lose' a thousand.)

Being a "Player" is Overrated

When growing up, playing wo/men sort of rocks. But as time goes by; one realizes that getting multiple orgasms from multiple sources seldom build empires, bring contentment, or, change the world.

So, the next time that you, and, your small-minded 'boys' or 'girls' brag about how you are sleeping with twins, and, how neither of them is aware; ask yourselves this question: what will you have to show for all your "playing," after, say, a year or eight, of sleeping around, used condoms, or, empty boxes of "morning-after" pills?

Are there any "praise worthy" fruits that you're reaping today, because of the countless partners that you have slept with yesterday?

Prostitutes are probably the only people whose sleeping around is putting food on the table. And that's only because an orgasm — or rather: the pursuit of one — is at the core of their making a living.

So, what happens to your dream while you are busy licking one of your sleeping partners' toes, or, putting your 'tongue' in their ear?

(The player is the only person that the player is playing. Seeing that it's easier for an achiever to play; than it is for a player to achieve.)

Rather Be, Than Have

In our times of materialism, many a people are caught up in the rat race. We have made 'having' the basis of our identity; to an extent that a man who has nothing, is regarded as nothing. And yet, we are surprised by the widespread presence of 'greed' within society.

The challenge is that 'being' is not really 'visible' to the rest of the world. That person sitting next to you in a taxi won't really be able to see "peace of mind" — should you be in such a state. But they will definitely see that $200,000.00 platinum watch on your wrist.

As a result, people would rather have a Ferrari than inner peace.

In his remarkable book, *To have or to be?*, Erich Fromm says that we're so obsessed with having; that we go as far as saying that a man has an erection. He then argues that the sexually excited man does not really <u>have</u> an erection — his penis <u>is</u> just in such a state.

Invest as much time, and money, as you possibly can, in who, and what, you are. Not what you have. Because 'things' come and go.

The very first generation of the iPhone rocked. Well, that was until Apple introduced the 2nd generation. But, within a year, the third generation took the "coolness" away from the 2nd generation. To-day, the 4th generation makes the third appear ancient. However, the fourth generation, too, will not be "cool" for a very long time.

A writer 'appreciates' with every single word that she writes; while her pen 'depreciates' with every word it writes. In short, the things that one <u>has</u> depreciate by use — while what one <u>is</u> grows by use.

If your lover is in your life only because of your deep pockets; what will happen to him, or her, should your pockets get shallow? Aha!

Er, ... I am fully aware that inner peace cannot really get one from Point A to Point B. And, in addition, regardless of their signature red; Ferraris are not evil. There is nothing wrong with having an abundance of material possessions. Provided that the things that you have are not the basis of your identity, a means to be socially accepted, or, your only reason for being, or not being, happy.

(One might lose their 'job' as a writer. But they can never lose the "writer in them." As one <u>had</u> the job; but <u>was</u> and still <u>is</u> a writer.)

Everything Depends on Something

In this world of ours filled with opinions, subjectivity, and relativity; it is either everybody is "right," or, every single person is "wrong."

Though in most cases I decide not to say it; whenever I'm asked a question my mind prefixes "Well, it depends ...," to my responses.

"... Is this a good logo?"

Well, that depends on the objective of the design brief.

"... Do I look good in this?"

Well, that depends on your definition of good-looking.

"... Is a Range Rover expensive?"

Well, that depends on the depth of your pockets.

"... Is a branding strategy necessary?"

Well, that depends on your definition of a necessity.

"... Are your offices far from the mall?

Well, that depends on how far is your far.

For one might be of a normal height to people in one's neighbourhood; but be regarded as a dwarf on the other side of the world.

(In the same way that the salary that Neo earns on a good month, might be less than a tenth of what Thabang makes on a bad day.)

Seven Minutes Past Too is Time

The present, the now, is the best time to do or create. But we are somehow programmed to start working from this-or-that o'clock or half-past this-or-that hour. But, what is wrong with starting your day's work at thirteen-minutes past, or to, this-or-that hour?

A Friend Gave Up on His Dream

Er, a friend of a friend has recently given up on his dream. How I wish that he chose to give up on giving up. His dream could still be.

Futile States of Mind

To be fearful is human. To worry about how things could turn out is human. To be stressed out is human. To be anxious is human.

But none of these states of mind makes a difference, not even a minuscule contribution, to what was, what is, or, what will be.

(Er, ... care to name a few things which you've changed or avoided because of how 'worried' you were about you not being able to?)

"If you worry about what might be,
and wonder what might
have been, you will ignore what is."

— Unknown

Fluency ≠ Mastery, or Intelligence

While at a friend's graduation, six or so years back, we were introduced to some young black lady who had "a white accent." She said, "Excuse the pun ...," about eight times every eight minutes.

Nothing wrong with that. Except that there was not even one pun in the "nonsense" that took her most part of the evening to utter.

There was this other guy we were with who was impressed by her "intelligence." Merely because he knew not what a pun was. So, he thought that she was 'intellectually' his superior. But, that was until I told him what a pun is. And that her rants were "punless."

Not every 'black person' that "sounds like a white person," when they speak English, makes sense, or, is intelligent. And, not every intelligent black person "sounds white," when they speak English.

I've actually met innumerable intelligent black people who cannot construct even the most basic English sentence, to save their lives.

A black female friend of mine says that she will never date a black man that is not "fluent" in English. But isn't that like a singer that can't dance saying that she'll never date a dancer that can't sing?

In a word, to know one's way around a design software does not necessarily make one a great designer. Just like how knowing one's way around 'pen + paper' does not really make one a great writer.

(Being familiar with a "kitchen" does not make one a good cook.)

The Length of Sleep is Irrelevant When One's Bed is Broken

Sleeping for less than the "recommended" eight hours a day is not the end of the world. It's actually the beginning of a "longer" day.

Quantity has forever been an illusional measure of quality.

A creative or a thinker's worth should be judged by the quality of their idea — not by how long it took them to conceive the idea.

Writing for 98 hours won't really make the writing superior to one that was written in 2 hours. An idea that took 30 days to think of, will not necessarily be superior to one that came after 3 minutes.

The best idea is so because it is unsurpassed. Not because its conceiver brainstormed for a few seconds longer than the runners-up.

(At times, I had ideas for designs which ended up being approved by clients, way before the briefing sessions were adjourned. Such cases are a paragon of the downside of billing clients by the hour.)

Life is Like Soccer, Everybody is a Coach

Generally, soccer fans think that they can do a better job, than the coach. Similarly, most people, around you, think that they know, better than you, what's best for you. And that's merely because ...

... things usually look way easier than they actually are, from afar.

Bills: Paid by Passion

Although it usually takes longer, before it pays dividends, the most fulfilling way to make money is by doing what you truly love doing.

Whatever it is that you find fulfillment in doing, irrespective of the financial gains that it might (or might not) yield, is probably what you were meant to bless the world with. Every single person has a purpose to fulfill. Alas, ... barely a handful pursue their passions.

Without a doubt, almost all "extremely wealthy" people have acquired their wealth doing what they're really "passionate" about.

Find something that you really love doing. Learn as much as you possibly can about it. Spend as much time as you can doing it. Be as remarkable as you can be at it. Make a difference to people's days or lives. And, inevitably, you'll find a way to make a living out of it.

Remember ... a paparazzi is merely an extremely nosy nobody that has a camera, and, "bills to pay." That, in a way, proves that every single thing under the sun, when one is not lazy to think, or, to be the first to be, or do, has the potential to earn one a dime or two.

(I mean, somebody woke up some day, and, they decided to monetize an orgasm. And then "bang!" Prostitution was "invented.")

The Price War Won't Get You Far

Being the cheapest is usually a hint of not being the greatest. The great compete on greatness, while the mediocre compete on price.

Even though it might seem "clever" to win customers based on affordability; being the cheapest is a short-term strategy, because there'll forever be someone who is willing to be cheaper than you.

That will either be because such people are willing to settle for a smaller profit margin. All in the name of luring your customers to their business, or, that they have cheaper suppliers. Meaning, they can be cheaper, but still make the same, if not more, profit as you.

A business's loyal customers should be, because of the value that others aren't providing. Not because the business is the cheapest in town. Otherwise, those customers aren't loyal. They're just broke.

(All that a dancer owes those in need of a dancer, is to be a great dancer. Not to be the most affordable dancer in the yellow pages.)

The Self-Esteem Deficit

Without doubt, people with a "high enough" self-esteem are rare creatures that the world will forever be under a supply of. A low self-esteem is one of the culprits behind the prevalence of trends, mediocrity, conformity, and, the worshipping of "the status quo."

I hold low self-esteem accountable for almost all underachievers' being. People with a low self-esteem find comfort in the safety of fitting in. As a result, geniuses are suffocated by such uniformity.

Like I always say, I would rather be ~~left~~ wrong alone; than be right with everybody else. That there is an imperative attitude that one must have — before one even thinks of 'challenging' convention.

(With a sufficient supply of self-esteem; one rarely gives a damn about what "other people" will say about them; should they fail.)

To Catch a Fish, First Study Worms

We are, in a way, all "marketers." Seeing that we are forever selling somebody something. Be it a product, a belief, or, an opinion.

Before one attempts to catch fish; it would help for one to familiarize oneself with how to catch worms. It is only then that one can "realistically" start dreaming of having "fish and chips" for lunch.

When a branding and a marketing strategy is not led by human psychology; the odds of the business "making it" are minimal.

We all interact with other human beings from time to time. Therefore, knowing how the human beings' mind works, is one of the most valuable assets to anybody who markets to such creatures.

Let's play a game to illustrate my point; visit ah-damn-and-if.com, and then go through the brief idea behind the movement.

Now, I challenge you not to think of AH, DAMN & IF™ whenever you see both, or either of, the two toilet icons; especially those on public toilets doors. If you see the toilet icons and still manage to not think of AH, DAMN & IF™ — then I would have 'lost' the bet.

Because I would have lost; I will then owe you. Either a big warm hug, or, a firm handshake. That'll highly depend on your gender.

It is not that it is impossible for you to see the toilet icons and not think of AH, DAMN & IF™, the challenge is that you'll have to remember to forget, for you not to think of AH, DAMN & IF™ then.

Yet the only way to realize that you have managed to forget, is by remembering; which will then bring what you forgot to mind. And also, you are much likely to think of me, or at least this book, every single time that you see, "Stars and Stripes," the American flag!

"Being a blockhead is sometimes
the best security against being cheated
by a man of wit."

— François de La Rochefoucauld

Don't Judge What I See Through Your Eyes

Granted, Kojo's dream of being the twentieth person to go to the moon is likely to be harder to accomplish; than Lesedi's dream of going to Ethiopia. But that does not make Kojo a better dreamer.

Kojo's dreams are not Lesedi's, and, Lesedi's dreams are not Kojo's.

That unemployed homeless pedestrian might actually be successful. Successful at whatever goals that she has set for herself. And, that overweight man might actually love being "abnormally" big.

Watching TV, or, doing absolutely nothing, might actually be the most productive thing that that person that you have already labeled as a time waster, could be doing at that moment, under his or her circumstances. Circumstances that you know nothing about.

So, I might actually prefer brown bread and baked beans over sushi — the best dish in the world; in your world. And, I might be deeply in love with the very same person that you so passionately hate.

(That is to say, do not force your fondness of pink skinny jeans on others. They might not like the colour pink, let alone skinny jeans.)

The Paradox of Enjoying Life

Being able to let go of "tomorrow's" worries, because today has its own worries, hints wisdom, and, it is vital for one to enjoy life.

One has to live within the present and stress not about the future.

While, on the other hand, to be, say, financially free "tomorrow," demands that one "sacrifice" the fruits that one could be reaping today, in return for a "more" fulfilling, and, fruitful "tomorrow."

"I Believe in You ..."

In our world of dreamers, entrepreneurs, and hustlers, "I believe in you ..." is as powerful, if not more, as the phrase, "I love you ..."

So, I would rather have someone tell me that they believe in me, rather than them tell me that they love me. Simply because, the phrase "I love you..." will not really encourage a dreamer to hold on, when facing challenging times that all dreamers are prone to.

Self-Employment is for the Lazy

One of the very first things that comes to almost every employee's mind, when he or she thinks of self-employment, is, waking up at 11 a.m., starting one's day's work at 2 p.m., or, not working at all.

Looking at myself and the self-employed people that I know; the opposite is true. Self-employment is not a remedy for hard work.

(In actual fact, some of us work harder and longer than most employees, their bosses, and, their personal assistants, put together.)

Social Media Anonymous

Facebook is, without doubt, one of the best online tools that one can use to search for long-lost friends, and, ... ahem, ... ex-lovers.

One of the basic human desires is to be, or, to at least feel, important. That is what made social media's success such a "runaway."

Apart from the fact that such websites give even the "uncoolest" kids of them all, an opportunity to be heard, and, maybe a chance to prove their coolness; it makes people who do not feel appreciated "offline," feel appreciated, and, that their 'opinions' matters.

Things like "retweets" and "liking" of someone's Facebook status update does wonders to the "liked" or "retweeted's" self-esteem.

Let me not get started on what the number of one's "friends" or "followers" does to the followed, or, the befriended's ego. Social media also gives people an opportunity to make social statements.

Some people subtly, and at times unconsciously, do that by sharing photos of themselves at such-and-such cool, or, expensive places. That's how people make social statements. By publicly mentioning, or showing, people that they hang with, the places that they hang at, the colour of the bottles of their beers of choice, etcetera.

By the same token, websites like Facebook affords people an opportunity to hurt their ex-lovers; by publicly stating that they are in an "open relationship." Even when they are still sans a better half.

Unappreciative other halves are losing the "attention" from their unappreciated other half, to websites like Facebook. While innumerable employers are losing money as a result of employees who abandon their work in pursuit of an ego stroke from their online "friends." Most of which they've never met, and, will never meet.

As a result, more and more unappreciated people, and, those who are declared as 'uncool' offline, are getting addicted to social networking websites. One status update, and, one tweet at a time.

While at a bank, three years back, the teller that was handling my application for a new bank card, switched from whatever program that they use at that bank, to Internet Explorer. She then browsed one of her Facebook friend's recently uploaded photos. That was an activity that she was clearly busy with, way before she looked at me, and then yelled, "... Nnnnnnnnnnnnext!" She did that while she waited for the bank's too-slow-for-her-liking system to "load."

Not to sound like a prophet wannabe, or, anything like that. But I think that there will be a need for rehabilitation centres that treats "Social Networking Sites Addictions." In the not so distant future.

The sad part is that, the majority of the friends that people make online are way too "insincere" to deserve the title of a "friend."

Lebogang Nkoane, a friend of mine, once 'faked' it. His birthday, that is — not stuff that some "unsatisfied" grown-up women do.

Like I was saying, Lebogang Nkoane did a little social experiment, via Twitter and Facebook. His birthday is on July 15th, but for his experiment, he faked his birthday. Not once, but twice. Lebogang's so-called Twitter and Facebook friends then wished him a happy birthday on the two faked birthdays — May 15th, and, June 15th.

Lebogang concluded the experiment with the question, "How social are these social networks? When the same people, still, wish you happy birthday on two wrong dates, separated by a month?"

Things are so bad that there are probably instances where while some half is busy whispering sweet nothings and moaning, "Who is your daddy?" in bed; the whispered to is busy wondering how many people could have 'retweeted' the tweet that she tweeted thirty-three seconds before the commencement of their foreplay.

("Hi, I'm John, and, I'm a twitterholic ...," will soon be an intro of some; at rehabilitation centers that we are soon to be in need of.)

Atheists Are Confident That Christians Are Lost

Generally, people are confident that they are right. And that whoever that's unlike them (be it their beliefs, their looks, or, how they see the world) is wrong, disorientated, or, not "seeing the light."

I'm convinced that atheists are confident that Christians are lost; as much as Christians are confident that atheists are hopelessly lost.

And, in our world of subjective reality, perception is more powerful than reality. Seeing that reality is nothing but how one perceives whatever that is in question. We trust a "qualified" medical doctor's opinion over that of an "uneducated" traditional healer; solely because we perceive the doctor to be the expert, thus, more knowledgeable and trustworthy than the "unschooled" healer.

And, because of nothing but perception, the "schooled" appear credible; while the "unschooled's" opinions are rarely entertained.

When arguing with someone you're likely to be confident that you are right, and, that they are wrong. While they, on the other hand, will be as confident as you, if not more, that the opposite is true. That they are "right," and, that you are so not "seeing the light."

The f.Law of Democracy

Even though "the majority" is nothing but what one is left with, after one has divided a population into two groups ... taking one person from one group, and, then putting them into the other. The group which the "votes" make "the majority," are given the power to select a few people who will then lead the entire population.

Yet, when "everybody" is put together, they are only as intellectual as the least intellectual members of the collective. It seems fair on face value, but isn't an average person average, intellectually? Or else, that would mean that any random ten people, when put together, are intellectually superior to Albert Einstein. Which I doubt.

The majority of the majority are average intellectually, thus, easier to be manipulated by second-rate politicians. So, a political party run by "fools" can use the people's money (read: tax) to hire one intellect that will persuade "the majority" to put, or to keep, the fools in power. What's more, the vote of a well-informed 90 year old carries the same weight as that of an "ignorant" 18-year-old.

(That is to say, in a country of three, the choice of two insensible people is not necessarily the best choice for the remaining sensible person. In most instances, it is not the best choice for all three.)

The Well-Paid Are Too Paid

People have a habit of drooling over how much so-and-so is paid.

People are open-mouthed by, say, a soccer player that earns, say, £11.3 Million annually. These awestruck people somehow tend to fail to remember that behind an employee is an employer, who, without a doubt, makes way more than the employed is paid.

Although, people who pay people who are well-known for being well-paid, love being behind the scenes, praise should be given to he who signs the cheque — not he who the cheque is signed to.

"If work were so pleasant, the
rich would keep it for themselves."

— Mark Twain

A Branding Testimony (via Soccer)

I don't know of the criteria used, or, the rituals people perform to help them choose a soccer team that they'll be an avid supporter of. But I for one was subtly persuaded by my dad to support Kaizer Chiefs — from the onset — until the end of my soccer fanaticism.

Fans embody brand loyalty, being the first, and, being the best.

In almost all cases, a soccer fan decides on a team to support, and, they then stick with it through thick-and-thin. The team would go through consecutive "dry seasons" — but the fan would remain.

(Ahem, ... well, most "diehard" football fanatics do stay around.)

What's more, every single fan believes that their team is the best team in the league, and, that those who support other teams are not "seeing the light." The same happens in the world of brands.

Someone tries brand so-and-so for their first time. Be it by chance, or, through a recommendation. More often than not, that person is likely to stick with that brand 'till death, or, unemployment, do them part. There are Zune owners, who afford an iPod, who are "convinced" that they have the best portable digital music player.

It's better to be perceived as the best, than to be the best, and, it's better to be the first, than to be the best. Seeing that branding is a game of perceptions, not reality. Branding is more about experiences, which lead to emotional attachment, than being 'the best.'

If "the best" is what soccer fans are really after; then they would change teams, in favour of the winner, at the end of every season.

Er, ... Once a pirate, always a pirate?

Top Students Make Great Employees

Like I said, you didn't really need to be intelligent for you to be a top student. All that you had to do was to forget the least in a test.

In addition, most of the things that educational institutions feed students are made of proven facts, thus, the past. The date which Jan van Riebeck was born will forever remain the 21st April 1619.

School populates students' minds with what happened yesterday, but rarely with what the students can do today or tomorrow. However, if all that you excel at is the known; then you will inevitably embrace convention, while your former "dumb" classmates change the world — for they find dates, the past, and, "facts" boring.

The majority of the people who give former top students employment are former "dumb students." Dumb students strive to build empires; while top students strive to climb the "corporate ladder."

(Generally, employees have better maths marks than their employers. It seems like courage is more profitable than a good memory.)

Sellers and the Sold To

All that radio, television, and, magazines were invented or created for; was to sell you something. So, make sure that the 'value' that you get from, say, a magazine, or, a television show, outweighs whatever that those who 'profit' from your "attention" will make.

Words That Made You Buy

Though we'd all like to believe otherwise; the majority of our purchasing decisions are mostly driven by emotions, not logic. Below are a few words that marketers rely on, to subconsciously get you to buy even things that you really do not need — let alone want.

Save, Proven, Guarantee, New, Improved, Trust, Deserve, Investment, Results, Free, Vital, Easy, Value, Proud, You.

By merely putting "Sale" on a product which's price isn't really reduced; sellers manage to get people who didn't go to the shop to buy "whatever" that is on sale, to buy "whatever" that is on sale.

Diamonds Are Polished, Not Found

We would all like to work on the perfect project, with the perfect client, that has a perfect budget. Alas, that almost never happens.

One mostly gets a perfect project with a perfect client that has an imperfect budget; a perfect project with an imperfect client that has a perfect budget; or an imperfect project with a perfect client that has a perfect budget. And there are more possible combinations (project, client, and, budget) that this can be expended into.

What makes a remarkable creative remarkable; is their prowess to get as close as possible to — if not surpass — the client's objectives — with the resources (tools, time, and, budget) available to them.

A client with a blank cheque kills creativity. Seeing that the medio-cre creative that the client appoints can 'outsource' the work to a remarkable creative behind the client's back; and then simply put a markup on top of whatever that the remarkable creative charged.

(Any "dull project" can be turned into a 'remarkable' project. it is all up to you. Go ahead, change the world with a grand or two.)

The Hustler's Guilt

When you spend a lot of time begging for food; you are likely to eat whenever you're offered food. Even when you are not hungry.

Usually, it is boys that chase girls. Hence, in cases where a girl likes a boy, and, she's woman enough to tell him; the guy submits. Even when he is not into the girl. Most guys feel like it is their problem when a girl that they don't like, likes them. So, when a chaser is chased, he thinks that he owes the then chaser to be caught.

Spam is Wasteful

Spam is a waste of the receivers' time and a waste of the sender's optimism. Rather market to ten thousand people who are in need of your product — than to a million random 'uninterested' people.

Ahem, ... that should be left to radio, and, television advertisers.

(Spam wastes two of life's most valuable things: time, and, hope.)

Un-Breaking News

With my getting rid of my TV came this question, "So, where will you watch the news?" That led me to 'answer' the question with a question, "What value does 'the news' really add to my life?"

Whether we are conscious of it or not, deep down we think that not being "up to date" with the "current affairs" will make us appear boring, weird, ignorant, "uneducated," or worse, "stupid."

In spite of the fact that I totally "disagree" with that, I sort of understand were "we" is coming from. But when was the last time that your up-to-dateness with the current affairs was questioned, needed, or, useful to you — or to at least the people around you?

Not that I don't sympathize with the people who lost their loved ones in that plane crash. But, in almost all instances, your awareness of such an unfortunate incident makes no difference to you, or more importantly, to the family or friends struck by the tragedy.

The *New Oxford American Dictionary* defines "News" as "Newly received or noteworthy information, especially about recent or important events." Now, questions is, whose definition of newly, noteworthy, recent, and important, are news providers using?

... Mine, yours, ours, "the majority's," or theirs?

News providers sort of dictate what you and I have to know, and, the sad part is that, like I said earlier, positivity doesn't sell. So, good news to us is bad news to the news provider's shareholders.

And, what does that mean for those who consume "the news"?

More and more negative stories are fed to them daily. Simply because all the bad and negative stories assure news providers an asset you have that pays their bills; your overly fought for attention.

News providers find stories that will captivate your attention. They then use that to get advertisers to pay them a fortune. By subtly feeding you whatever it is that the advertisers want to sell to you.

I am not fond of scheduled content, as in almost all cases, it forces the publisher to always have something to publish, come d-day.

Has there ever been a day where your news provider went like:

"Sorry, there are no 'news' today. Thus, we have nothing to say."

I doubt it! News providers must always have something to say. To them, always having something to say is golden, and, silence isn't.

I stopped watching and reading "the news" for a month; just to see if I'd wake up someday, only to find that everybody went to a safer place, after news providers warned them about something terrible that just happened. Something that my ignorant and stupid decision not to watch or read the news made me miss.

... And? (Drum roll) ... Zilch! Nothing! Nada!

I don't remember who did; but someone once said that newspapers should only be read at the end, not the dawn, of one's day; because you would be depressed all day. I saw sense in that, but I took it a step further; by intentionally not consuming news at all.

Let's take the BP oil spill as an example; did your awareness of the oil spill make a difference to your life? Did you make a difference to the oil spill? Isn't knowledge supposed to be acquired with the intention of using it to do something useful at some point in your life? What did you do with your (then just acquired) awareness of the oil leak? As a people — do we merely know, to merely know?

If a South African's "unawareness" of the colour of the dress that Jacob Zuma's fourth wife wore to his fifth wedding, makes them ignorant, stupid, arrogant, and, uneducated ... then, I plead guilty.

"My doctors told me this morning
my blood pressure is down so low that
I can start reading the newspapers."

— Ronald Reagan

Divided We Stand, United We Fall?

Generally, two underrated "individuals" make an overrated group.

When coming to novel, avant-garde, unorthodox, and, unconventional ideas: the more people that an idea's approval depends on; the less the chances of being brought to being the idea will have.

Almost anyone can easily push a brick to whatever direction that they wish to. Nonetheless, with every brick that we add, to unite with that one brick, the harder it gets for one to push the bricks as a collective. That there is the beauty, power, and, purpose of unity.

However, when coming to individuals and society:

One plus one *plus* one is, at its most, equals to one. In most cases, it is equal to less than one.

Society somehow encourages its "members" to strive for nothing but acceptance, comfort, and, security. What's more, people were brainwashed to use the "average" of the society as a benchmark.

Society, an aggregation of human beings, somehow manages to weaken the individuals that collectively brings it to being. As a collective, the world asserted that conveying people through the air was impossible. So, should the Wright Brothers have been foolish enough to entertain that; airplanes would still be a pipe dream.

The more people there are in a person's environment; the more susceptible that person will be, to the opinions of "the majority."

Er, ... Divided we stand, united we fall?

Branding
Misunderstood

First thing first, a product, or a company's logo, is not a brand.

A brand is the "perception" that consumers have with regard to a company and its products. It is what the consumers see it as. Not what you say it is, or, desire it to be. Meaning that consumers, not companies, "define" brands. Generally, as per their perceptions.

People have too little time, and way too many choices, of products with similar quality or features, sold by way too many companies.

A branding promise is the reason other than price that companies use in their attempt to lure prospects to buy their products or services. For different people prioritize different things when buying.

The first thing that some people demand in a car is safety. Such people will, in all probability, find a Volvo more desirable. In the automobile industry (and in the minds of many consumers) Volvo owns the word "safety." Yet Volvos are not necessarily the safest cars in the marketplace. What matters is the perception held by consumers; not the scientific certification that BMW might have.

In branding, and, in marketing, it is better to be perceived as the best, than it is to actually be the best. It is the consumers' perceptions about "brand x" that leads to them buying "brand x." Not the verifiable fact that "brand x" is indeed better than "brand z."

Being the best in an industry isn't enough. It's merely a good start.

What's more, a branding message requires patience and repetition for it to be tattooed in the minds of consumers. Thus, branding is not for shortsighted entrepreneurs that seek overnight successes and instant gratification. No amount of money can buy one time.

Wine is a "perfect" example. The quickest that a wine cellar can produce an eighteen-year-old bottle of wine; is in eighteen years.

Family is Underrated

I may have never met you, your family, or your friends. I might not even know of the dream that you're busy chasing. But whatever it is; achieving it at the expense of your loved ones won't be fun.

Rather a failure with family and friends; than a lonely 'successful' person. I don't know about you; but the bank notes that I have bumped into so far, do not give hugs. Not even on your birthdays.

So, do chase your "dreams" with caution, and, consideration.

(Er, ... if growing up means not seeing one's family on the regular; all in the name of paying the bills. Then grown-ups are overrated.)

The Tooler Fooled by the Tool

Some creatives incl. the phrase, "Made on a Mac," when show-casing their work; especially on their website. I think that, that is nothing but a symptom of one hiding behind one's tools of trade.

A great book is exactly that — a great book. Whether it was written by hand, or, was typed on the world's most expensive laptop.

The world only cares about the greatness of a painting; not about how 'shallower' the painter's pockets were left; after she bought the paintbrush, the paint, and, the canvass. Come to think of it, the tools that a writer writes with, are none of the readers' business.

A recent iMac using creative — that works in a fancy urban office, won't necessarily produce work that is superior to — a Pentium II PC using creative — that works from a shack — in a township.

(The taste of the tea matters more than the kettle it was boiled in.)

The Virgin Active Irony

I was in a taxi when I realized that the fat driver was wearing an equally oversized golf T-shirt which had Virgin Active's logo. A few gear changes along the line, I thought to myself, "… but that's like seeing a homeless person wearing RE/MAX's promotional T-shirt."

(Nothing wrong with that; ambition is a precious commodity.)

Anyhow, … as the taxi driver did what he does best, beat robots, I started to find Virgin Active's plus-sized promotional t-shirt a bit ironic — but more disturbingly — self-contradictory.

Wouldn't it be foolish for a school that is attempting to lower the number of students who bunk school — to offer free merry-go-round rides at the park — during school hours? Wouldn't it be childish for a parent who wants to coax their kid to eat healthier, and less junk food, to double the kid's allowance in such a pursuit?

What is the best thing to buy for one's overweight couch potato best friend? A skipping rope, or, a more comfortable couch?

Wouldn't it be more encouraging, and fruitful, for one to buy their size thirty-four friend — who wishes to lose weight — a size thirty — and not — a size thirty-four pair of pants?

I say Virgin Active should exclude plus-size, and, smaller oversized T-shirts from their promotional T-shirts campaign orders. And then, they should deliberately handout smaller T-shirts to overweight people — people who it is evident that the T-shirts will not fit.

Image what would go through the mind of an overweight person that seldom thinks of losing weight; when he finds out that that T-shirt that he so liked doesn't fit. The smaller T-shirt will push him to reflect on his weight. And that is likely to hint and encourage weight loss; while subtly reinforcing Virgin Active's brand message.

If the overweight person does not keep the small T-shirt for their ideal slimmer self; he is likely to give it to someone that he is sure the T-shirt will fit. So, Virgin Active will not really be losing a prospect — they will actually be gaining one more billboard on legs.

By accommodating plus-sized people in their promotional T-shirts, what Virgin is doing is comparable to a 'Quit Smoking' brand that gives smokers free lighters; hoping that they will use their brand.

The f.Law of Yesterday

Because of man's desperate desire to foresee things; he habitually, and, painstakingly, study yesterday in his attempt to foretell today.

But, the fact that one hasn't successfully swam yesterday, and the days before that, does not necessarily mean that one cannot swim today. So, one should never say that she "cannot" do something. Rather she say that she never did something "successfully," as yet.

If You're Waiting to Be Found, to Be Lost You Are Bound

The only person that has one's best interest at heart — is oneself.

A lot of what could have been "classic books," were also buried, when their authors were laid to rest. Merely because some publishers were of an opinion that the books were unlikely to sell.

(... the huge impact that opinions of small-minded people have!)

As sad as it may sound, people who finance an artist's art, or, an entrepreneur's dream; do so, solely because they're almost certain that the artist, or the entrepreneur, will make them money; not because they think that the artist is talented, friendly, funny, or, cute.

Most business associates would have never given most artists their time of day; should they have not been convinced that there is money to be extracted from the in need of money artists' art.

When a client hires a consultant, the client is not really doing the consultant a favour. In the same way, an employer hires an employee with certainty that the employee will make the employer more money than what the employee demands, every four weeks or so.

Let's not allow the paychecks to fool us. Nobody is doing the other a favour. An employment contract too is a "business transaction" that is presumably a fair deal to both the seller, and, the buyer.

In the same way, a client will either hire a creative because the creative produces remarkable work, or, merely because the creative is the most affordable in town. Either way, the client will not really be doing the creative a favour, should she decide to hire the creative.

(Unless the dream that you need money or help to realize promises to benefit he or she whose help you seek; you are on your own.)

"Everyone is a genius. But if you judge a fish by its ability to climb a tree, it will spend its whole life believing it is stupid."

— Albert Einstein

Expensive is Double-edged

More often than not, the asking price is the only barrier between a prospect's wallet and the entrepreneur's bank account.

When a prospect that was astonished by a product ends up not buying the product, solely because he thinks that it is expensive; his definition of, and what lies at the core of, his "expensive," will determine who, between the two, is to blame for the lost sale.

If the prospect thinks that the product is expensive merely because he doesn't afford it; it is the prospect's problem. If he can afford it, but perceives it as exorbitant — it is the entrepreneur's problem.

To solve this issue, the entrepreneur needs to either: decrease the asking price, or, to increase the product's perceived value. The former needs a calculator; the latter requires a remarkable marketer.

Entrepreneurs who suffer from the curse of instant gratification; people who unknowingly erode their long-term brand equity (all in the name of short-term returns) almost always opt for the former.

The Artist, Their Art, Critics, and, Groupies

What made the Mona Lisa, ... "the Mona Lisa"?

Was it the greatness of the painting, or, was it that the number of people who were of an opinion that the painting is a masterpiece outweighed the number of those who thought that the painting was not up to scratch, fair, not bad, so-so, or, just "OK"?

An applaud is a beautiful thing, especially when it is deserved. It is good for most artists' egos. But while it has the likelihood to draw more people to the art; it does not add anything to the level of greatness that the painting had after the artist put the last stroke.

The Mona Lisa would have been, and would forever be, (whatever that you think of the Mona Lisa), even if Leonardo remained the 'only person' in the world to ever lay their eyes on the painting. Remarkable things remain remarkable; whether we applaud or not.

So, after the art is concluded, the only thing that art appreciators might change is the depth of the artist's pockets, his popularity, his ego, and, maybe his chances of getting laid; but not the art itself.

This writing is, (whatever that you think of this writing), whether you speak well of it or not — and it would've still been, (whatever that you think of this writing), should you have not read it at all.

(All that criticism and "groupism" change is the artist, not the art.)

I am a Genius

... And so are you, the next person, and, the person next to them.

Every single person has a purpose to fulfill. Sadly, most people are not willing to spend the time (and the money) required to seek what it is that they were brought to being to bless the world with. Would Michael Jordan be declared as remarkable, should he have decided to be "an accountant" — primarily to "... pay the bills"?

(Every single person is a "genius." The world is just crowded with dancers that play drums, and, drummers that dance to pay rent.)

The Refuge for Nonsense

We, as writers and speakers, like to send impressions that make us appear more intelligent, "dope", or, "deep," than we actually are.

Nine times out of ten, our "choice of words" seems like the easier route. And, as a result, people who should have kept their mouth shut hide their reasoning, with little or no meaning, behind words.

Similarly, designers hide meaningless designs behind complexity.

A complex word that is used in place of a simpler synonym is only excusable if, and when, it adds value (be it rhetoric, or, otherwise) to the spoken or the written — otherwise, it is merely a show off.

Politicians are notorious for relying on bombast to either impress people, or to hide the insignificance of their promises. But question is, what is the use of deliberately confusing the very same people that you are trying to communicate a message, or, a promise to?

That is to say, when engaged in a conversation, isn't the listener's understanding of the spoken, the speaker's responsibility?

Generally, the things that takes a politician two hours to say, could have been said in 15 minutes — the things that takes a mediocre writer a book to express, could have been expressed with a paragraph made of a hundred words, and, a brand's ten paged mission statement, could have been summed up by a remarkable slogan.

(No amount of "bombastic" words will add sense to a nonsensical sentence.)

As Predictable As ... ?
A Gospel Music Video

Music videos are one of the most boringly predictable creations. All that a gospel artist need is a backdrop of a river or a mountain, ideally both, and then, they're ready to rock 'n roll. As opposed to the typical hiring of a crowd, tons of makeup, few attractive women, kilometers of fake hair, and, semi-dressed women — things that most music videos' chances of grabbing attention depend on.

We're All Judgemental Creatures

We subconsciously "filter" people we meet, and, we mostly use their appearance to decide whether we allow them into our lives or not. Be they our friends, ~~family~~, employees, better halves, etc.

The very same manner in which we assume whether someone is trustworthy, or, of the remarkable quality or professionalism that they claim to be — occurs in the world of business and branding.

A fashion designer with garments that retail for thousands of dollars; but has a logo, business card, marketing materials, or a website that looks cheap; is the epitome of self-contradiction. That too is comparable to a broke financial advisor — or an extremely overweight fitness instructor that goes around yelling the importance of exercising to any prospect that gives him or her the time of day.

(The style of writing in an ad, the colour scheme of a website, and, the choice of typography, subtly "says a lot" about the business.)

Sleeping for 8 Hours is Overrated

It goes without saying that sleeping is a great way to rejuvenate. But it is, for the most part, overrated. We do not all work equally hard, yet we are all advised to rest for an equal amount of hours.

It is a brand new day, and, that means that one has been blessed with yet another day to live. And what does one do?

He spends a third of the day "playing dead." Sleeping it is called.

That then means that a man that has slept for 8 hours a day, since birth, would have slept for exactly ten years, on his 30th birthday.

Life is a temporary gift; thus we should try to be awake for as long as we possibly can, throughout the journey. Seeing that there will be more than enough time for one to rest ... once one is no more.

The Anatomy of Effective Design

Graphic designers use the visual arrangement of a layout to either present content, communicate a message, or to do both. And, in the context of things like CD covers — the design is the message.

But it's only when the arrangement of the contents affects what it conveys, that the design and the message can be regarded as one.

When drinking tea, you don't necessarily think, "Oh, I'm drinking hot water, sugar, milk, and crushed leaves." As you would be see-ing them as you should — as a collective. The same applies when a viewer consumes a design. They don't necessarily see: the album's title, the artist's name, and, their portrait — they see a CD cover.

In some cases it is the photograph that carries the intended mes-sage. So, question is, do we give credit to the photographer, or to the designer; merely because she arranged where and how the photograph is placed? And, if the message is communicated by the typeface, who gets the credit? The designer, or, the typographer?

The end product is one, and, for that reason, the message and the design are one. It's only when the designer has failed that viewers consume the design as the multiple elements that makes it whole.

The design is the sole mode by which we consume the message.

(We see parts of a design as a collective. A design should be seen as a collective. As a thing, not an arrangement of a group of things.)

Abundance Dilutes Value

Society rarely values an artist's art while the artist is still alive.

But once the artist is no more; one starts seeing or hearing the art-ist's art everywhere that one goes. That there is 'scarcity' at work.

People generally value things that are difficult to get. Be it because of red tape, a premium cost, or, a limited edition. I actually think that the quickest way for an artist to sell their art in large numbers or at a high cost is to either die, or, to fake their own death.

(Ahem, ... If you're to opt for the latter; do warn your loved ones.)

"Every society honours its
live conformists and its dead
troublemakers."

— Mignon McLaughlin

The Irony of "Supportive" Friends

An entrepreneur that sells a product for a hundred dollars is likely to be expected to sell it for forty dollars to her family, and, friends.

Apparently, that is all in the name of her family, and, friends being "supportive." But that's not really support; that's called a discount.

Furthermore, this thing of buying a product from someone solely because they're your friend, or a family member, is so last century.

And, believe it or not, that is also detrimental to the entrepreneur.

It is potentially harmful in a sense that even an unsatisfactory product will be bought. And, that dramatically reduces the odds of the entrepreneur being aware that her product is substandard.

(Er, ... I pray that my nearest and dearest will read this book solely because they found it insightful; not merely because I authored it.)

Start Your Day the Night Before

Starting with the day's work, the night before, is arguably the best way to produce one's best work. All that one has to do is a to-do list. If you are going to, say, be writing; write a few headlines, or topics that you're going to write about. And that's about it! Go to bed. And let your subconscious mind do all the working, while you are asleep. You will thank me, come lunchtime, the following day.

The f.Law of Averages

On average, an "average person" is average. Average in terms of capabilities, tastes, expectations, demands, dreams and standards.

"Many", "most", "more", and, "the majority," has for long been used as a measure of a creation, or, a deed's greatness, and, merit.

So, if the readership, or, the number of a publication's subscribers, is a true measure of the quality of the writings; then not all great writings will produce a large number of readers. And, not all writings that manage to impress a large number of readers, are great.

So, in a way, the worth of a doer, a writer, or, a performer, is in the hands (or rather: in the minds) of the done for, written for, or, performed for's standards, tastes and expectations. A person with average thinking capabilities will find a thought-provoking writing intimidating. And, as a result, they will find the writing "boring."

Democracy too relies on the greatness-by-numbers mentality when appointing a president. But, not every great political party will get a chance to rule. And, not every political party that rules is great.

Take a look at the people that your art appeals to; their standards and brainpower are a true measure of the quality of your art.

Whether or not 'grilled chicken' is better than worms; in terms of both taste and nutrition. A fish is more likely to be seduced to the hook by a worm. Not grilled chicken. I mean, what's the use of grilling the poor chicken, if all that the poor fish want is worms?

So, that is to say that the Average Joe's art is not as remarkable as he thinks, desires, asserts, or, assumes. His art merely conforms to average people's average brainpower, and, average expectations.

Brands Hate Employees

Like I said earlier, even the most remarkable branding strategy will take some time before it starts to yield returns. On top of that, nobody will really care about a brand's future more than its owners.

Here is what typically happens to brands:

A board of directors hires a brand manager. Let's call her Joan.

Joan makes decisions that yields short-term returns at the expense of the brand's long-term equity. Three years later, Joan leaves the company. A successor is hired. Let's call him Lebo. A year later, the damage caused by the decisions that Joan took four years earlier, is starting to weaken the brand's equity, and eventually, its profits.

Joan got paid, and, she moved on with her life. Lebo, her poor successor, gets the boot. As it seems as if he is the incompetent one.

A brand should be managed by people who honestly give a damn about where the brand will be in 20 years' time. Preferably, people who would either be dead, or, still part of the brand by then.

The Meaningfullessness of Words

Er, ... Lady, or, gentleman; I present to you: (drumroll)

A B C D E F G H I J K L M N O P Q R S T U V W X Y Z

… the alphabet — a standardized set of letters in a fixed order — used to represent the basic sound of language.

Show them to any random person, and they are, more often than not, unlikely to mean anything to them. Seeing that they do not really communicate, express, mean, or, "say" anything.

(Obviously, … they will remind some of us of the crush that we had on our third grade English teacher — but, such is life.)

And, what happens when we rearrange and reuse some of them?

The alphabets now have the potential to give birth to words like:

Nigger, bitch, coconut, whore, loser, jerk, fat, useless, kaffir, failure, crow, boer, chonky, coolie, flip, half caste, nip, motherfucker, cunt, fatherfucker, fool, brotherfucker, bastard, sisterfucker, moron, idiot, dummy, arsehole, brownie, blockhead, et cetera.

And, all of a sudden, those "meaningless" letters are now capable of evoking emotions out of whoever that they are directed to.

And, at times, the emotions that these words induce, are so strong that people end up reacting in ways that they would not have, should they have not been offended by such words.

But words only mean what we allow them to mean to us.

The next time someone uses such words, with an attempt to put you down. Just think of the alphabet, and remember how meaningless the letters are when they are on idle. Your reaction, or lack thereof, will disappoint he who uses such words to put you down.

Calling a cat a dog doesn't really make or change the cat. So, why be put down by being called a fool, a nigger, a loser, or, a kaffir?

While the offender needs to offend to be. Reality is that, … to be offended is the choice of the offended.

(Er, … the above sentence was the end of this writing … "loser!")

Power Naps Are Profitable

Well, that will depend on the kind of work that the business's employees are employed to do. If it's thinking that's at the core of the workers' bread and butter — then 'power naps' will yield returns.

Instead of 'forcing' an evidently fatigued creative to work for, say, eight hours — hours in which the creative will undoubtably be unproductive; rather allow the poor creative to sleep for two hours — and then let him or her work for the remaining six hours.

The standard of one's ideas, and, the value that they add, should not be judged by how long has one slaved. If it is productivity that you value — allow your creative team to take a power nap or two.

(Nothing is as profitable as a refreshed and well-rested "thinker.")

Asking for Budget: To Milk, or Not to Milk the Client

How much will it cost to build a house that's big enough to house a man, his wife, seven offsprings, and, twenty-three grandchildren?

That there is an example of a typical question that entrepreneurs demand a quick answer to — from "poor" consultants.

In non-tailor-made instances, where things are ready-made, that question could be answered with ease. But even two competing businesses in need of, say, a website or a branding strategy, will have challenges and needs that are exclusive to their business.

That is to say, it rarely takes the same amount of resources to design, say, brand identities for competing brands, e.g., BP and Shell.

The most important resource in any project is the client's budget.

Seeing that it dictates how much of this-and-that and how many hours of doing this-and-that will the consultant be afforded in his or her pursuit to get as close as possible to the project's objectives.

I have a 'very simple' modus operandi. I ask the client to enlighten me as regards their business, competition, project's objectives etc., and the maximum budget that they afford to invest in the project.

I will then decide whether what the client would like to achieve is feasible when weighed against the budget at the client's disposal.

Generally, the buyer pulls out all the stops to pay the least that the seller could possibly settle for. While the seller attempts to sell for the highest price that the buyer can afford. Sadly, this has programmed entrepreneurs to assume that whoever that asks how deep their pockets are (maximum budget) is trying to milk them.

Most entrepreneurs think that if they mention that their budget is, say, $1000 — then the consultant will then charge them $999.98.

Chances are that a builder can build a house for, say, two hundred dollars. But if she who seeks a house can afford to pay a thousand dollars; then the builder should build a thousand dollar house.

In a nutshell, a car salesperson can definitely get one a good car. But the car which the salesperson can recommend will highly depend on one's needs — but more importantly — on one's budget.

(Almost everything is achievable when one has a "blank cheque.")

"To be great is to be misunderstood."

— Unknown

Kwaito Artists Can Be So Lazy (And Untruthful)

" ... Monday. Monday, Tuesday. Tuesday. Tuesday, Wednesday. Wednesday. Wednesday, Thursday. Thursday. Thursday, Friday ... "

Add to that — a beat and a husky voice — and you'll have one of the songs that kwaito once populated the airwaves with. And like most kwaito artists tend to claim; the artist is likely to assert that he was inspired by South Africa's "diversity." Nothing wrong with that. But I think that the poor calendar also deserves some credit.

That brings Francois Marie Arouet's comment on singing and the sung to mind, "Anything that is too stupid to be spoken is sung."

(Ahem, ... not all kwaito songs are about the "days of the week.")

Respecting "The elders" is Overrated

Being old, or older, is not really an "achievement." All that an old man had to do to be "older," is to not kill himself. Seeing that off-springs don't really contribute to their making or being. And more importantly, they have nothing to do with "when" they are born.

So, even if a woman does nothing but sit on a street corner for 80 years, from the day she was born, she'd still be 80 after 80 years.

(To hell with age, race, job titles, background, education, financial and social status; respect should be given to every single person.)

Thinking
Inside the Box

School has programmed, say, designers, to solely be interested in design, design books, design topics, and, design issues. It's rare to find a designer reading a philosophy, geography, or, science book.

Yet there are so many non-design-related theories, and elements, that designers can take from, say, science; which they can incorporate into their design solutions. So, when brainstorming, look for "inspiration" from industries, or disciplines, other than your own.

(You're free to reside in a box; just don't think after-hours. People who only read [enter a profession] books are boring after-hours.)

Dreams Are So
Overrated

We all have dreams. Most people have unexceptional, but expected, hence "safe" dreams; while a few dream "impossible" dreams.

But having a dream is easy, but, that should not be where it ends.

Contrary to popular belief: a dream isn't a true measure of a man, what he makes of his dream is. If he who has a "bigger" dream is better, then whatever that your dream is — I want twice as much.

So, does that make me a better dreamer than you? I think so, not.

It is a dreamer's actualization of their dream that differentiates an achiever from a dreamer — not the size of the dreamer's dream.

If all that Bill Gates did was nothing but parade his dream; Windows OS would still be nothing but a dream. By the same token, if all that Alexander Bell did was dream, without taking action to make his dream a reality, the post office would still be profitable.

The difference? The two "former dreamers" took action.

Dreaming, like talk, is cheap. I think that Benjamin Franklin said it beautifully when he said that "Well done is better than well said."

Being "a dreamer" is a beautiful thing. Provided that that 'title' is temporary. If all that you do is dream, without taking action, you'll forever be dreamer. But that will not change anything, or, anyone.

Dreams, like knowledge, are worthless without action.

(Thomas Alva Edison's dream for a lightbulb was only "worthy" of praise after he succeeded in making candles appear "old school.")

A Salary Rarely Builds Wealth

Come to think of it ... it never does. The prevailing habit of trading one's time for income, a day for a day's pay, never creates wealth.

If it is wealth that you are after — I am afraid that the security, the comfort, and, the predictability of a salary will not get you there.

All that a salary can do is to ensure that you sleep on a full tummy, have a roof over your head, and, that you get into debt with ease.

Wealth is built through passive income. And that's money that you make without trading your time, or, you having to be "there."

Moreover, employed rich people aren't rich; they just have expensive cars and big houses. Things that they would not possess for long, should they not be paid for a month or three. That is owing to the fact that they owe what they foolishly think that they own.

Comedian Chris Rock joked that, "Wealth is passed from generation to generation. You cannot get rid of wealth. Rich is something that you could lose with some crazy someone with a drug habit."

Design is Underrated

Design made you choose some product over another. Design gave you an order without saying a word — toilet icons. Design, book cover, is the reason some people gave this book a browse; which led to some of you buying it, and then, reading the entire book.

(The challenge is that, to be effective, design has to be unnoticed.)

The Laughing Lady at Checkers

While at Checkers, some young lady laughed at some guy, who had no underwear underneath — after she realized that his pants were unzipped. I found that a bit silly. I mean, what the hell was she expecting to see after looking at the poor guy's groin? An ear?

Reality is in the Eyes of the Perceiver

What is reality? Is it what the majority of the people say it is, how "the majority" perceive the world, or, how you perceive the world?

Is a red car red because most people perceive it as red, or, because it is indeed red? Is it still a red car to a person that is colour-blind?

Maybe HIV does cause AIDS. But how many of those who believe that it does, have proof that supports such a "belief"? Almost all people who do, do so merely because they perceive the doctors that assert so to be learned experts — hence, trustworthy and credible.

A large number of what we assert to be real or truthful is made of things that we have not personally proved or experienced. Yet most people can bet with their lives that the earth is 4.54 billion years old. Moreover, even if we had the privilege to see, say, a 'scientific fact' being proven; it is the perception that we had regarding the credibility of whoever that did the test that made us buy their assertion.

(At the core of what we believe to be 'the truth' lies a perception.)

When Life Gives You Shit

Life can be hard. Pessimists call it a bitch; optimists call it a journey.

Either way, life had, life has, and, life will forever have, challenges; both big, and, small. Regrettably, that is how we acquire wisdom.

It is because of yesterday's scars that one will be able to steer clear of tomorrow's wounds. Life is beautiful. What isn't, is how people who think otherwise choose to look at it. Perception, perception ...

There is always something valuable to be extracted from whatever, good or bad, that is placed on your path of this journey called life. So, ... the next time that life gives you shit, worry not. For there is manure to be made. It all depends on he who the shit is given to.

Jack of Many Trades

School has programmed human beings to believe that "the most" that one person can be, is to be just one thing. One is either an artist, a scientist, a marketer, an architect, a receptionist, or, the like.

Still and all, I believe that one person can do or be all of the above all at the same time. And still be remarkable while they are at it.

There are gazillions of things, apart from golf, where greatness and stardom could be realized. Is a golfer the only "thing" under the sun that Tiger Woods can be, and, be remarkable at? I doubt it.

Being a great writer is not the end of the writer's greatness.

Not everybody's greatness + talents are limited to just one métier. Also, I'm not fond of being labeled this-or-that. I'm whatever I say that I am — not what a piece of paper (read: qualification) asserts.

I am only "qualified" as a graphic designer, but I also love and do: writing, copywriting, designing user-interfaces for websites, marketing, photography, branding strategies, and, a few other things.

I see myself as more than 'merely' a graphic designer. In fact, to be nothing but a graphic designer would mean that I'd be using less than a tenth of my talents and creative (and thinking) capabilities.

I am by no means a Jack of all trades. I am merely a Jack of many trades, who happens to master all that he trades in. I know that that is counter-personal-branding's rule of thumb; because being a lot of things makes it harder or even impossible for someone to be known as, or for, something. But it is the paintings that I paint that I wish to spread, which will lead to them being known of; not me.

Granted, specialization has its own pros. But, despite that, not every person that does only one thing, is remarkable at what they do.

Nina Simone was a singer, pianist, arranger, civil rights activist, and, a songwriter. And guess what? She too disliked being categorized.

(Go ahead. Be a remarkable entrepreneurial accountant that paints amazing paintings when he or she isn't fiddling with a calculator.)

The f.Law of Statistics

A statistician is merely someone who desperately tries to foretell tomorrow by painstakingly studying yesterday to pay today's rent.

The fact that someone saw the last twenty years doesn't necessarily guarantee that that person will see the coming twenty seconds.

Furthermore, ... if yesterday was that important, it would still be.

While today might be of the same name as the day that was upon us seven days heretofore; today isn't that day. As a people, we are so used to being alive -- that we fail to be thankful for being alive.

"Man must not allow the clock and the calendar to blind him to the fact that each moment of his life is a miracle and a mystery."

— Herbert George Wells

The Powerfoolness of Media

The media is arguably one of the most powerful man-made entities in the world. The media shapes perceptions of the masses; while it subtly defines their definitions of subjective things such as beauty.

The media has subtly caused not-so-skinny women to come across as not-so-beautiful: in the eyes of the magazine or remote holder.

The media has the power to help a non-profit organization raise funds to save trees, pandas, and, starving kids in Africa. It also has the power to depress the masses by continually feeding them bad news which their consciousness of won't really make a difference.

The media has the power to prompt a beautiful black woman to find herself unattractive; unless she suffocates her beautiful black skin with makeup, and, hides her beautiful black hair with weave.

I think that black women who still find themselves beautiful without fake hair, or makeup, are an endangered species. I think they need to be celebrated. Those in a forest sans the media are lucky.

Malcolm X, an enfant terrible which I hold in high regard, famously said that, "The media is the most powerful entity on earth. They have the power to make the innocent guilty and to make the guilty innocent ... and that's power. Because they control the minds of the masses." Another commentary on the media that I like was uttered by "Unknown," and he or she said that, "The people who own the mainstream media are manipulating public opinion to conform to their objectives. There is a reason TV is called PROGRAMMING."

The only "choice" that the masses have is over who to consume the news, edutainment or gossip from; not what their medium of choice feeds them. The same applies with magazines, radio, and TV.

Work for 8 Hours, but Bill for 24

In the creative industry, and, other industries, where one's job entails "problem solving," through the generation of ideas; most of the work — brainstorming — is done when one is not "working."

People who work for other people call that period "after-hours," which unfortunately, is time which most employers do not pay for.

Our subconscious mind is, in most cases, the culprit that manufactures ideas that help us pay rent, and, put food on the table.

And, as you might know, we do not really have control over what goes on in our subconscious mind. The closest that we can get to controlling our subconscious mind, is by influencing it through the part of our mind that we have control over, the "conscious" mind.

Almost all remarkable ideas were conceived while one was in the shower, while taking a walk, or while watching a movie. But rarely in a cubicle while one is desperately trying to come up with ideas.

For ideas knows no working-hours, working days, or, holidays.

The best way to solve a problem is not to think about the problem. Well, not "consciously," that is. Allow the poor client to brief you, promise them heaven and earth, call it a day. And then ... (Ahem)

Go for a walk, go to gym, go plant a tree, go cut a tree, go watch a movie, go make a movie, read a book, write a book, go start a party, go end a party, listen to music, make music, do something, or, do nothing, go wherever, or, do whatever — anything but work.

(Whether he's at home or on holiday; a thinker is forever on duty.)

"Expensive" is Defined by Returns

What makes a product, or a service provider, expensive?

What makes a $98,000 website, or branding strategy, expensive?

Is it 'realistic' for a penny-pinching entrepreneur to demand, or to expect, a $100,000 return; be it in cash or increased brand equity; from a project where the entrepreneur paid (read: invested) $500?

Is "expensive" dependent on the prospect's bank balance, or, is it dependent on the returns that the investment promises to yield?

Paying a consultant $100,000 for a two-hour consultation session sounds "expensive." Well, ... that is until finding out that her insights will yield a return of, no less than, a hundred million dollars.

... And then, all of a sudden, her fee sounds like a "bargain."

For as long as a twenty million dollar pair of socks will make way more than twenty million dollars for the entrepreneur that bought the pair; then the poor exorbitant bundle of wool isn't expensive.

(Entrepreneurs need to stop "whining," and, start "investing.")

The Artist Doesn't Make the Art

Our creations matters way more than we, as their creators, do.

Would "We are the world ..." kindle the same set, and, the same amount of emotions, in whoever that listens to it — should the song have been sung by the Soweto Gospel Choir and Trompies?

Would you get the very same effect, or affection, from the Mona Lisa — should the painting have been painted by Gerard Bhengu?

Whatever it is that you get from this writing; would it have been different, or the same, if this writing was written by someone else?

Between the Mona Lisa and Leonardo da Vinci, who made who?

(Leonardo da Vinci might have created the Mona Lisa, but the Mona Lisa made Leonardo da Vinci, "Leonardo da Vinci.")

Corporate Social Irresponsibility

If you give some random homeless person a rand — are you then going to go around yelling, "I just gave some homeless person a rand ..." to every single person that cares enough to lend an ear?

A gift is only a gift when it's given out of will and love and without the expectation of a return or an applaud. Otherwise, it is merely a business transaction, or, a marketing tactic for the desperate.

Brands that ran out of "tactics" to acquire new customers, or, to increase costumer loyalty, think of corporate social responsibility as a quick "wangle" to please their not-so-pleased shareholders.

Donating one million dollars to an orphanage is a beautiful thing. I honestly think that it is. But then — after doing so — why tell me?

If all that you did was 'donate' money, and then, the transaction ended there — what difference will my awareness of such a transaction, or donation, make to me, to you, or, to the "donated to"?

You donate a million dollars, and then, spend nine million dollars on an "advertising campaign" that yells about how much you just donated a million dollars to such-and-such an organization.

If the money that you just donated to the poor-kids-sans-parents was an honest gift like you so desperately want the entire world to believe. Instead of donating one million dollars and then spending nine million dollars on a campaign that yells about you having donated one million dollars — why not donate ten million dollars ...

... And then, shut the hell up?

(That would mean less noise for us; and more money for the kids.)

The Stove Calling the Fridge White

I wanted to put myself to sleep. And, I thought to myself, "What better way to do so, than to watch TV?" So, I watched TV. I then ran into an interview of one of South Africa's renowned designers.

Amongst other things — he ranted about how South Africans are reluctant to pay 2 thousand dollars for a garment; while the very same reluctant South Africans willingly pay the same amount, if not more, for garments made by "international" fashion designers.

He pleaded with South Africans to let go of the perception that internationally produced products are superior to those made locally. ... Nothing wrong with that. Actually, I am of the same "opinion."

Although he kept on mentioning the word 'branding' during the course of the interview — I think that his plead shows how clueless he is on branding -- a discipline that he passionately spoke about.

Diesel is solely responsible for whatever perceptions that consumers have regarding its products. Such perceptions were brought to being by Diesel's deeds, or lack thereof, not consumers, or, Levi's.

Branding is all about manipulating the perceptions that consumers have regarding your products or services. If you make remarkable products; but for some reason consumers see your product as second-rate — you only have yourself to blame, not the consumers.

Without a doubt, the designer interviewed makes "world-class" garments that are worth every single cent that he charges. But his corporate identity and website shouts "cheap," an image that contradicts with his intended, and, desperately desired, brand image.

He has a cheap logo and a cheap website; things that are usually the first thing that his prospects see. Yet the very same "cheap" marketing collateral are expected to sell "expensive" garments.

How satisfactorily, or not-so-satisfactorily, that a brand is perceived is the brand owners' problem — not the perceivers'.

In the context of logos, corporate identities, marketing collateral, et cetera — design acts as a means to visually clothe brands. And like with people, brands are initially judged by their "appearance."

This is yet another example of a great product failing to realize its full potential because of a third-rate, or lack thereof, branding and marketing strategy that is coupled with third-rate graphic design.

Although I sort of understand where he was coming from — the famed fashion designer's plea to South Africans is an exemplar of hypocrisy at its peak. He presents his brand in a "cheap" manner; yet he complains that his garments are perceived to be overpriced.

(People in glass houses somehow find delight in throwing stones.)

"If you don't read the newspaper,
you are uninformed; if you do read the
newspaper, you are misinformed."

— Mark Twain

Doers, Believers, and, Witchcraft

The things that we receive are merely fruits of our deeds; not because we believed that we'll receive whatever that we're receiving. The cause of this misapprehension is that we do because we believe and we believe because we did. Do students pass exams cuz they studied, or, merely because they believed that they will pass?

Did they perhaps believe that they will pass because they studied?

Life has its own rough patches, challenges, and, misfortunes. We "acknowledge" them, learn from them, and then, we move on.

But should one, for whatever reason, start believing that they are bewitched; those rough patches, challenges, and, misfortunes — things that one used to learn from, and then, move on; will now appear to be a 'confirmation' that one is indeed being bewitched.

(Have you ever wondered why the new word that you just read up on, all of a sudden, appears everywhere? That there is the result of "selective attention." WYGIWYS? What you get is what you see?)

An Ego Boost, by Social Media

Facebook is useful for finding long-lost friends, and, ... ex-lovers.

One of the basic human desires is to be, or to at least feel, important. To a large extent, that is what made social media such a hit.

Apart from the fact that websites like Facebook and Twitter afford even the "uncoolest" kids of them all, an opportunity to be heard and to prove that they are actually cool. They make people feel appreciated — and that they, their lives, and, their opinions matters.

Things like "retweets" and the "liking" of a Facebook status update, does wonders to the liked, or, the retweeted's self-esteem.

Let me not even get started on what the number of "friends" or "followers" does to the followed, or, the befriended's self-esteem.

Social media also gives people an opportunity to make social statements. Some people subtly do that by sharing photos of them at such-and-such cool or expensive places. Social media also affords bitter single women an opportunity to hurt their ex-boyfriends. By falsely and publicly stating that they are in an "open relationship."

~~(That's how some people make social statements. By publicly showing off the people that they hang with, the restaurants that they eat out at, the colour of the bottles of their beer of choice, et cetera.)~~

Rappers Suffer from Vanity

Yo! Some rappers don wanna grow up. Know what I'm saying? Er, ... you can call me a hater later. But for now, allow me to explain.

Music is an extremely powerful communicative tool. Nonetheless, innumerable rappers fail to use even a quarter of its full potential.

You're 40, yet you still rap about how many women you can sleep with in a day; how many times you can change clothes in a day, without exhausting your wardrobe; how cool, deep, and dope you are; how many cars with 20 inch rims you have — and how much of a "dangerous" emcee you are.

Do you honestly think that I should spend my hard-earned money on an album made of songs where you talk about nothing, (with the exception of "women", "cars", and, "haters."), but yourself?

I think such rappers are too big for their boots. Or, better still, silly.

Come to think of it, such rappers should actually pay us listeners to listen to such useless senseless gibberish that happens to rhyme.

The only time where an artist that only "talks" about nothing but himself, is excusable — is when whatever that he says about himself will somehow add value to whoever that listens to such songs.

Instead of taking an entire album to hint that you have deep pockets, you could have just tweeted that you're well-off. Rather than recording eighteen songs — just to announce that you are loaded.

It Takes a Day to Meet a 24-hour Deadline

If this project is due on the 19th of May, why should I have it ready before the 10th of May? A silly question that we often ask ourselves.

Have you ever wondered why it normally takes you two weeks to complete a project which you were given two weeks to complete?

Well, within *Parkinson's Law*, Cyril Northcote Parkinson maintains that work expands as to fill the time available for its completion.

... So, take a project that usually takes your team six days to complete. Tell them that that project is due in three days. And then watch how their day's "productivity" will seem to have doubled.

Never Read a Book Once

To get the most out of a book; read it more than once. For 1 great book has the likelihood of changing one reader more than once.

As readers, we, more often than not, judge, and, comprehend, a book based on what we currently know — and do not know, our current level of thinking, our current intellectual capacity, etcetera.

With the passage of time people grow (well, most do). In terms of brainpower and what they know. And, it goes without saying that those with a passion for reading grows quicker — and more often.

That means that you are likely to "better understand" the writings in a book after re-reading the book; a few months (or years) after your initial reading of the book. In addition, you are likely to agree with writings which you initially disagreed with — or better still — disagree with writings which you have initially blindly agreed with.

At times, you're likely to grant some authors less respect than you initially had for them. Because after reading some books — you would have bumped into writings which the authors that you so esteemed "borrowed" — without crediting their original authors.

(Until you "disagree" with at least one author whose writings you initially agreed with; you haven't done enough reading ever since.)

Esteem by Medium

Generally, the "credibility" that people give to, say, an opinion, is mostly dependent on the medium used to share such an opinion.

A book is arguably the most credible medium. But I'd hate for you to blindly take the things that I rant about in here — without scrutinizing my points of view. There are probably writings in here that you agreed with, which you would've disagreed with, should they have been 'said' to you — as opposed to being 'printed' in a book.

At the end of the day, authors are human. Their opinions just happens to be inked on paper. They too are not immune to fallibility.

(In a nutshell, judge what is being said by what is being said; not by the medium that she who said it, used to say the said.)

The Irony of Sung Heroes

Suppose that there's a small remote poverty-stricken village somewhere. All that the villagers know is the village. No one in the village has a job; nor have they ever owned, let alone seen, a bicycle.

By chance, Titus, a nobody in the village, goes out of the village.

He 'bumps' into a mine, placed in a small town, a few kilometers from the village. A town that nobody in the village knows about.

He then sees a conspicuous "We are looking for mine workers. No qualifications, or experience, required!" notice on the mine's gate.

He goes inside. He is told that an ID is all that they will need from him. And, without hesitation, he produces his ID - and hired he is.

Titus is then begged by his new boss to refer people that are looking for a job to the mine — as there are still a lot of 'vacant' posts.

He moves into a flat in town. Time passes. He realizes six paydays.

Titus is now doing well, financially. He then buys himself a bicycle. He becomes the first person in the village to see and own a bicycle. He goes home. On his arrival, he is treated with respect. Suddenly, the kids in the village wants to be "like him" when they grow up.

Before he worked at the mine, no woman would give him the time of her day. But all of a sudden, Titus is now on a lot of women's lips. Both, figuratively, and, literally. Titus is now "the in thing."

Now, how likely is it that he will tell his fellow villagers about how he got the job — something that enabled him to buy the bicycle?

The dilemma is that he knows of a place where the majority of the men in the village can get a job — like he did. As he was told that the mine is in need of more employees. But, on the other hand, if he refers the men from the village to the mine, his extraordinary achievements will soon "appear" ordinary. Owning to the fact that most men will then have a bicycle and a job at the mine.

As a result, Titus will not be praised anymore. As a matter of fact, chances are that Titus will then be a nobody — like he used to be.

People are sort of fearful of helping others, mostly because their success will mean that theirs, something that only they have realized, will be realized by many. Meaning, they won't rock anymore.

And like it happens in economics, abundance dilutes value.

If a commonly ridiculed person is suddenly praised by a thirsty nation, merely because he's the only one with a bucket full of water; do you think that he would tell such a nation where the well is?

(The irony is, of course, that it is the people's praising that makes the praised; yet their praising is the reason that the praised will not tell those that are doing the praising about what made the praised worthy of their praise. Because once they too are praiseworthy, the praised will be just another person that has what everybody has.)

"You don't win silver, you lose gold."

— Nike's '96 Olympics slogan

Businesses Are Run, Not Planned

Business plans are like statisticians, they desperately try to foretell the next year, by painstakingly studying the previous years. Yet it only takes one tiny out-of-the-entrepreneur's-hands thing to shatter a business's financial projections, expectations, and aspirations.

... things like the economy, market conditions, competition, etc.

But before shredding your business plan; I think it will be unfair of me not to alert you that I am a broke entrepreneur. So, such an ignorant attitude might be the cause of my two-digit bank balance.

Business plans exist merely to give us an illusional sense of control.

The Complexity of a Sale

One of the hardest (and, in most cases, impossible) things to measure accurately, is the return on an investment made on design. Be it an investment on brand identity, product, or, packaging design.

That makes it difficult to sell the value of design to entrepreneurs.

It is extremely difficult to sell someone something; if you cannot measure the return that that something will yield, or if you cannot even provide them with some sort of "results." To overcome this challenge, companies that sell lose-weight-without-a-sweat products rely on 'Before-and-After' photos to build credibility, and, to ultimately persuade consumers to make that sale.

I have never been a woman, (duh!), but I've heard that the way in which a guy presents himself counts big time. The "presentation" is mostly made of the way that the guy is dressed, and, groomed.

Allow me to use a silly analogy to illustrate a point:

We have some guy walking in a mall. And, Bang! He sees a good-looking woman. A fitting potential daughter-in-law to his parents.

He makes a move. She ends up telling him her name.

From that scenario, it's unlikely that the guy will know what made the woman give him her attention, and, a chance for him to promise her heaven-and-earth, and, him climbing the highest mountain.

... Fast Forward. The guy and the woman are now dating.

For the guy's realizing of his ideal ending — do we credit the way that he was dressed?, his looks, or the "Your father must be a terrorist, because you are the bomb!" lame pickup line that he used?

Could it be that the emotional state that the guy found the girl in played a part in her agreeing to date him? Maybe she was just tired of being lonely, therefore, desperate for anything with two legs.

Suppose the guy is interested in having as many women as he can possibly get. And say he knew that he won all of his 10 girlfriends' hearts because of the way that he dresses — isn't it obvious that he'll invest more money on clothes; instead of wasting time memorizing 'cheap' pickup lines — because for him they bear no fruits?

Let's get back to business. (Business, ROI, and, design, that is.)

This analogy illustrates how difficult it is for a seller to know what had the sole or the biggest influence on a buyer's buying decision.

When a consumer buys a toothpaste from, say, Colgate, can we really measure what pushed the consumer to opt for that brand?

Could it have been the TV ads that the 'poor' consumer has been constantly fed? Or, could it be Colgate's new enticing packaging?

Could it maybe be that the consumer grew up in a household that used that brand religiously? Or, could it have been that Pick n Pay had an irresistible discount on Colgate's toothpastes that day?

... Or maybe, just maybe, could it have been that Colgate was the only brand in stock at the time that the consumer went shopping?

... Or better still, could it be that Colgate paid a premium for the premium "eye level" shelf space — the most selling shelve space?

Or, could it be because the toothpaste is a great product in itself?

A sales process is simple. A customer simply selects a product that they like, and, they then pay for that product, right? Yes, and, No.

Yes, that is a fairly simple procedure. And no, as their selecting of a product part is a bit complicated. That's where design, branding, marketing, sales, promotion, et cetera. — play an imperative role.

After a consumer 'acknowledges' their need for a product — they have to make a choice from hundreds, and sometimes thousands, of brands offering the same product with the same benefits. Let's make it more intense — brands competing for the same "wallets."

This is a stage where companies rely on branding, sales, marketing, design, etc. to make their actual product appealing to consumers. Because it usually takes more than one discipline to sell a product.

That is what makes it puzzling to measure returns from an investment made on design — and 'other' disciplines — for that matter.

When packaging attracts a consumer's attention, instill trust, and then, the consumer ends up buying the product. Who gets the pat on the back? The graphic designer or the store manager for offering customers a 50% off discount that day? Design does not exist in isolation. And usually when it contributes, usually the most, to a consumer's buying decision — marketers and salespersons (rarely the poor graphic designers) are given a warm pat on the back.

Seth Godin, a renowned marketer, maintains that "Marketers take a lot of credit — because marketing is near the end of the game."

No selling tactic exists in isolation. An intelligently designed packaging, or that remarkable slogan, might be the final thing that persuades a customer that was lured by a discount, to buy a product.

Being Famous is Hard

... Not that I am. But I find the thought of countless "thoughtless" people knowing about someone, their work, their opinions, their weaknesses, their love life, et cetera., a bit disturbing. The worst part being that when that famous person runs into any random person — they don't really know whether that "stranger" knows about them, their opinions, their work, their ex-lovers, or not.

I think that celebrities fall into either of the two types below:

The first type is made of people whose deeds, or words, changed other people, industries, or the world; hence it was 'unavoidable' for them to be renowned. These are my favourite type of people.

And then, we have people whose goal was merely to be famous; and what they are known for, does not really matter to this type.

The first type rarely act "celebritish." Body guards, glasses, and all.

One of my favourite quotes on famous people and fame is by Fred Allen — an American comedian — who "famously" quipped that — "A celebrity is a person who works hard all his life to become well known, then wears dark glasses to avoid being recognized."

Money is Not the Root for Some Evil

Kabelo did not have money for university, so he robbed a bank to pay for his studies; and Neo has been starving for a week, so she robbed a store, just so she could buy bread. Now, the question is:

What was the root for evil there; money, starvation, or education?

The Simplest Way to Attract Attention

With the exception of soldiers that are taking part on a battlefield, blending in is "deadly." Looking like your surroundings, or, those in it, is the culprit behind not standing out. The more similar that a thing is to its surroundings, the harder it is for it to be noticed; because people's brains are wired to adapt to consistent patterns.

As humans, our brains are designed to be conscious of change.

Likewise, any sound, regardless of how pleasant or irksome it is, will attract people's attention, in any space that's consumed by silence.

When attempting to grab attention with, say, a poster, instead of overpopulating the poster with meaningless trivial visuals that are likely to blur the message that the poster was brought to being to communicate; rather make the poster of a colour or a pattern that will contrast with the surface that the poster will be put on.

(Simply put, don't overburden the design. Simply break a pattern.)

Freezing Winter Nights, and, Hot Summer Days

The sowing that one does in the midst of today's famine, will lead them to tomorrow's plenty. And, the food that one wastes in their times of plenty, will lead them to tomorrow's famine.

That's to say, the wise things that people do during their bad times creates their tomorrow's good times; and the 'foolish' things that people do in their times of good creates tomorrow's bad times.

In his book, *Peaks and Valleys*, Spencer Johnson, well-known for his other book, *Who Moved My Cheese?*, says that when you're experiencing good times, it is your turn to enjoy life — and when you're undergoing difficult times, it is your turn to learn about life.

Stand for Something

Either that, or, sit for nothing. Same difference, don't you think?

It is "impossible" for an artist or their art to please, or, to even be understood by, every single person. Likewise, it is "impossible" for an artwork to be regarded as reasonably priced by all and sundry.

People, who disregard this truism, either paint second-rate paintings; just so that they also appeal to the not-so-intellectual people in the market. Or, they lower the quality of their art, merely to be 'affordable.' Those who don't stand for anything rarely say, "No."

(Being hated by someone is a sign of having stood for something.)

"If you don't stand for something,
you will fall for anything."

— Malcolm X

Weekends Are Overrated

Generally, people who love and "obsessively" long for weekends hate their jobs. Weekends are merely life's gift to such poor slaves; people who are enslaved by paychecks and the illusion of security.

As might be expected, such people are all over the place on weekends; the only time that they're free from the cubicle. You'd swear that that weekend is the last -- before the world comes to an end.

... Yet, there will forever be a weekend, come next weekend.

On the other hand, a Friday, a Saturday, or a Sunday, is merely yet another day to be thankful for, and, to try to get as close as possible to one's dreams; to people who do what they truly love doing to pay rent, esp. those whose employers and themselves are one.

If there are varying levels of one's zest for life, between weekdays and weekends; it's because one is forced to love what they do, as opposed to, doing what they love. For loving what one does demands that one love what they do; love that one might not have.

One Man's Misfortune Makes Another a Fortune

After someone has died, one gets two types of people. Crowds of people with tears of loss, and, a person, or eight, with tears of joy.

With every single second that goes by without someone dying; the harder business gets for undertakers. In the very same way, tabloids profit from "documenting" well-known people's misfortunes.

Like I said before, regardless of how useless the demanded might be; where there's a demand, a supply will forever be. So, while it's tempting to put blame on such journalists, people who study hard for years, only to write about other people's misfortunes and misdeeds, patrons of such publications have themselves to blame for being fed such junk that pollutes their minds with useless stories. 'Information' that they will not have any honorable thing to show for having known; in a year, month, week, day, or, an hour's time.

Question is, ... what do you have to show for your knowing of Tiger Woods' infidelity? Or that so-and-so broke up with so-and-so?

What value does one's 'awareness' of the fact that so-and-so slept with her girlfriend's younger brother add to one's life? Are we that bored as a people? Is gossip and the downfall of others so important that we line up in long queues on Sunday mornings — just to get an update of who did what, where, when, with, or, to whom?

Do people who profit from your interest in such useless "Breaking News" consume the useless junk that you so consume and spread with enthusiasm? Again, I doubt that those who profit immensely from cigarettes smoke. Do you think that drug lords take drugs?

(Granted, we cannot all be "producers." But that does not excuse being a foolish consumer. One can still demand a valuable return from everything that they consume and/or spend their money on.)

The Personal Trainer Dilemma

The longer that it takes a personal trainer's out-of-shape client to get into shape — the more money the personal trainer will make.

Likewise, the 'quicker' it takes an out-of-shape person to get into shape, the less money the trainer makes. Good news to a recently got into shape former overweight person is bad news to the personal trainer's bank account. So, trainers face a dilemma of having to choose between a fulfilled client and sleeping on a full tummy.

People Don't Fail, Methods Do

A very close friend of mine recently "failed." An exam, that is.

But instead of seeing himself as a "failure," as one would expect, he told me that he did not really fail. He maintained that it was the method that he used to study for that exam that failed him.

(Er, … he read that "somewhere." Dr. John Tibane's book, I think.)

I thought that that was a great way to look at a nonfulfillment.

I then wondered, "What if we took that attitude towards failure, a step further?" And then, after that, I imagined how much of a positive impact that that would have on learners, if this choice of how one perceives "failure" was used in our schooling system.

…. Imagine if school teachers gave marks to the students' studying methods, not the students themselves.

The good thing about such an approach would be that after one has "failed" the first thing to come to one's mind would be, "How could I better that method that has just failed me?," or better still, "Which method can I try next ?," instead of feeling like a failure.

That would, in a way, also dramatically reduce the number of students who commit suicide after realizing that they've not made it.

(Ahem, apologies to undertakers and people who make coffins.)

Instead of looking for less hurtful ways, or words, to blame themselves — people who just "failed" would inevitably seek solutions.

Over and above that, after someone has "failed," instead of them giving up on their dream; they are likely to give up on the method that has just failed them. And, ... they will then try again. Bingo!

(People do not fail, ... it is the methods that they use that do.)

A Blank Page: A Plagiarist's Worst Nightmare

I love Apple's products. I love beautiful things. I love reading books by Seth Godin, and, I loooooove looking at good-looking women.

But, nothing fascinates me more than a pencil, and, a blank page.

The brief aside, the 'creations' that could be created with a pencil and a blank page are only limited by the creator's imagination.

Still and all, plagiarists find a blank page intimidating. However, I salute emptiness; for it gives somethingness an opportunity to be.

The Mona Lisa wouldn't exist if it wasn't for a blank canvas.

While a block of wood might "dictate" what a sculptor can — or cannot — bring to being; a blank page is an epitome of freedom.

(Likewise, this book was at some point nothing but a blank page.)

iTunes Killed
Second-rate Songs

Generally, technology makes it "easier" for creators to create, and, more importantly, it also makes it easier to spread such creations.

Even so, on the other hand, the very same technological advancement makes it easier for pirates to be. Truth be told, I think that it sucks for an artist to work hard, only to have someone who didn't lift a finger make money from the artist's blood, sweat, and, tears.

(Ahem, ... now that we have got that out of the way ...)

The 'upside' of stores like the iTunes Store is that music lovers are no longer 'forced' to buy the entire album — in cases where the album, except for a song or three, is made of second-rate songs.

That is good news for music lovers, and, a good motive for artists to make albums made of first-rate songs. Songs worthy of a buy.

That also means that an artist, should they have some guts, could release a one-track-album. That one first-rate song alone, sold via iTunes, is likely to yield more financial returns, than a second-rate album sold the traditional way — as a collection of songs.

An album made of "remarkable" songs is likely to sell every single song — on the iTunes Store — so, there will not be any loss there.

For years, recording companies fooled, and bullied, music lovers.

Before, we were "forced" to pay for eighteen songs; even when it was only two songs that we liked. That was unfair because to love *"Speechless"* is not to love every single song by Michael Jackson.

(A new 'technology' rarely hurts artists who make remarkable art.)

Being Hated is Underrated

Love is one of the loveliest things that one can experience. Imagine "being loved" by every single person. That sure would be lovely.

But, when you fail to find at least one person that hates you:

... It is either you are doing what has been done, or, you are doing nothing at all; or it is either you are saying what has been said, or, you are saying nothing at all; or it is either you are travelling on a path that has been travelled on, or, you are not travelling at all.

People who worship the status quo only notice people who challenges it. And, eventually, people who challenge the proven, the known, the safe; make those who are comfortable with the safe, uncomfortable. That inevitably breeds hatred towards such beings.

As shocking as it might sound, even Nelson Mandela had (he probably still has) his own "haters." Owing to the fact that not everybody wanted what he helped South Africans realize to be realized.

(So, if there aren't any people who think that you suck, you suck.)

Miriam Makeba's Thighs

Selling is hard. Some people sell sex. While some use sex to sell.

I admire, and have respect for, musicians, males and females, who rely on their talent to mesmerize music lovers; not on publicly parading body parts that should be reserved for their better halves.

Regrettably, even musicians who have innumerable loyal fans, and more than enough money to 'self-publish' their albums, are subtly "dictated" to show more skin, and less silk, by their record labels.

Even so, the world was blessed with remarkable artists like Miriam "Mama Afrika" Makeba. Artists whose art contributed enormously to people's lives; while their thighs remained exactly that — theirs.

This widespread gimmick of undressed musicians, at its best, only attracts people to music videos; but it rarely leads to album sales.

Because, when on a CD, a song is listened to — not "watched."

Therefore, whether a song was recorded naked or not, sex has no power to sell, or to attract. Because it will just be the listener and what the song is conveying; not how close to naked the artist was.

Quarrels Are Two-Dimensional

More often than not, we take sides, in support of the person that told us about an argument, not the person that they argued with.

The problem is that people who tell you about an argument, tells it as per their 'perspective.' So, it is easy for you to hate someone solely because their perspective opposed, say, that of your friend.

... Even in instances where your friend is the one on the wrong.

(Your friend's, or loved one's, enemy isn't necessarily your enemy.)

"Everyone is gifted, but some people never open their package."

— Unknown

What is Being a
(Enter Job Title)?

In the context of work, and job titles, what exactly is "being"?

Am I a writer because I say that I am a writer, or, because you have been reassured that I have access to a pen and a piece of paper?

What makes a geologist, a geologist? Their "triumph" in studying and then recalling the dates and theories that they were fed by a textbook, or the mere fact that that person thinks that rocks rock?

Am I what I say I am, or, what the rest of the world and a piece of paper (read: qualification) say that I am? Is the labeling highly dependent on "the majority"? Am I what most people regard me as?

Again, ... is a red car red because most people see it as red, or because it is indeed red? Is it still a red car to a colour-blind person?

Is reality 'defined' by how the majority perceives the world? Is anything real so long as the majority of the people perceive it as real?

I say that a person is 'whatever' that they say they are. Seeing that being this-or-that is nothing but a reference to he who is; because being this-or-that does not make the referred to, the referred to.

So, I might have never fixed a tap; but should I call myself a plumber, a plumber I will be. I might have never been near a plane; but should I call myself a pilot, a pilot I will be. And, I might have never boiled an egg; but should I call myself a chef, a chef I will be.

If we are what we are as the aftermath of the array of skills that we were taught; doesn't that make an 'uneducated' person nothing?

(Go ahead, call yourself an astronaut; even though you have never even left the town that you live in. I will still take you "seriously.")

144

Awards Are Not the Beginning of the World

Awards are good, esp., for the awarded's ego, chances of getting laid, and, at times, their hourly rate; therefore, their bank balance.

Awards are awarded by human beings; and because of that, subjectivity is, more often than not, at the core of the judges' decisions. Over and above that, the more avant-garde, novel, and unconventional, the art is, the less the likelihood of the artist "winning."

And, at times, who gets what award is decided by "public vote."

... subjectivity, subjectivity, subjectivity! And, what's more disturbing is that people with little or no expertise in this-and-that decide who best deserves to be titled the year's "best this-and-that-er."

Yet, the "weight" of a compliment is dependent on how great he who compliments is on the complimented. So, not every underweight runner that's complimented by an overweight one is really a fast runner. Not everyone that is greater than someone is great.

Some judges' votes are lured by bribes; while some vote in favour of their friends. Scratch a buddy's back, and, he will scratch yours.

Sad to say, there are innumerable first-rate artists who have never won a single award, and, countless third-rate artists who are struggling to find 'space' to put their too-many-to-be-counted awards.

All that most awards do is celebrate 'the past' and/or trends; what is currently in fashion. That is probably why almost all unconventional artists are only celebrated decades after they have passed. Perhaps that is a fair "punishment" for being ahead of one's time.

Furthermore, most creatives are subconsciously trained to do work which they hope will please the jury. And, inevitably, such creatives almost always forget to sell what they were hired to sell.

The other issue I have with awards is that there always has to be a winner; which means that they don't necessarily award based on excellence, but the least-worst in that particular year and category.

Judging creative work has moved from the proximity between the brief and the creative solution — to pushing creatives to compete against each other. All at the expense of the poor clients' projects.

Yet, different clients have different business challenges. Thus they require different results from their collaboration with creatives. Plus they have different-sized budgets, resources, and, time frames.

How can two runners be regarded as competing; when one runs on a 400m track — while the other is running on a 1200m track?

If you want people to compete and to be judged fairly; give them the very same challenge, resources, time frame, and, suchlike.

(The creation of creative work is an expression; not a competition.)

Possessions Don't Make Their Possessor

We live in a world jam-packed with people who suffer from materialism, that we show respect (or lack thereof) towards each other, based on what we have, and, rarely on who we are. To materialistic people, which makes "most of us," our possessions makes us, us.

But shouldn't the possessor "make" the possession; not the other way around? Think, if you will, of the most expensive thing that you have ever bought; particularly something that gave you street credibility. Now, between you and the possession, who got who?

The Death of Interest, by Numbers

Like I said, we're all marketers, one way or another. Some people burn the candle at both ends — in pursuit of creative ways to sell products. While others work hard to 'refine' their rationale in their attempt to sell their ideas, dreams, or points of view, to the public.

When trying to 'amplify' the impact that your figures will have on people; instead of saying that 25% of the children die from starvation annually, which is a bit vague, rather be more 'dramatic,' and mention how starvation robs the lives of 1 in every 4 children, every second hour. The former is almost "impossible" to imagine.

... Or better still, focus on one individual that's suffering from, say, cancer, or, starvation; when attempting to get people to donate a dollar, or seventy, to your breast cancer, or malnutrition, initiative.

... Soviet politician, Joseph Stalin, said it better when he said, "The death of one man is a tragedy. The death of millions is a statistic."

(So, tell prospect donors about a starving kid, not a dying village.)

Constructive Criticism vs. Destructive Compliments

In this world of ours, a lot of things depend on a lot of things.

Was Michael Jordan a "great" basketball player? Is Mutabaruka a great dub poet? Was Ben Maraka a great comedian? Was Thabo

Mbeki a great president? Was Moses Molelekwa a great pianist? Was Fela Kuti a great musician? Was The Notorious B.I.G a great rapper? Is Vusi Mahlasela a great singer-songwriter? Is Steve Jobs a great CEO? Is Spike Lee a great film director? Was Mahlathini a great mbaqanga singer? ~~Is Mokokoma a great graphic designer?~~

... Well, that will highly depend on your definition of "great."

And, that will also depend on how you see them and their work.

Furthermore, while our premise (read: the definition of "great") — might be concurred upon, there is still plenty of room for our viewpoints to contradict. Subjectivity, subjectivity, subjectivity!

And, like I said earlier, subjective arguments rarely produce a gold medalist — since each contestant will also double as the "judge."

... Tell someone that their work sucks, that their looks are way below average (read: "ugly"), or, that their writings are second-rate.

... And they are very likely to reply, "... Well, that's your opinion!"

As defensive as that might sound, they are right, it is your opinion.

But why are we so quick to take a compliment; and then run as far as we possibly can with it, (just incase the person that has just complimented us changes their mind), the minute someone compliments us on our looks, work, talents, character, walk, talk, etc.?

Regardless of whether a criticism is "constructive," or not, it rarely gets the warm welcome that a compliment is sort of guaranteed.

So, how constructive is a compliment, in our world of subjective opinions? To this day, I am yet to hear a person that has just been told that they're, say, talented, reply: "Well, that's your opinion!"

The Affordability Guilt

Creatives are traditionally hired to come up with ideas that solves a business or a product challenge. And at times, a few proactive enterprising creatives convert ideas into products that they then sell.

But, either way, creatives are in the business of selling ideas. So, to put it in another way, a creative is a merchant of ideas.

Creatives sell ideas, not 'tangible' products. Moreover, to conceive an idea, a creative only needs one raw material. Time. Time is the foremost raw material that a creative needs to manufacture ideas.

But, regrettably, because "time" is all that creatives are required to spend — countless creatives inevitably "undervalue" their worth.

They charge for a day, what they should have charged for an hour.

"... Hey, I mean, I won't really have to go buy flour, oil, salt, icing sugar, garlic, eggs, or something of that sort, to design a logo for that bakery down the road. So, ... $30 ain't that bad, right ...?"

As a creative, I am what I am today, in terms of expertise, insights, and experience; because of sleepless nights, talent, and, sacrifices.

I love what I do and I'm not really in it to chase money. But please don't try to pay me as little as I can foolishly, or desperately, settle for. Esp., if you're using my expertise and insights to make money.

The problem with creatives is that they think that they're responsible whenever a client cannot afford their expertise. When a client cannot afford your expertise, it's not your problem, it's the client's.

(As I write this book, I am nowhere near affording a Ferrari. Now, question is — whose problem is it? — Mine, or Ferrari's?)

"Public opinion requires us to think other men's thoughts, to speak other men's words, to follow other men's habits."

— Walter Bagehot

"I am, Therefore I Think … "

I think that people who say 'Never say never' should practise what they preach. I think that **jazz rock**. I think that "deep down" every single woman thinks that she is blessed with either singing or modeling talent. Most think they possess both. I think that women who don't play hard to get are hard to get. I think that **condoms are the new abortion**. I think that wisdom is finding out that a cobra is deadly, without first having to lose one's life. I think that before saying something online, people should be sure that their opinion isn't temporary. For Google forgets not. I think that **marrying young is overrated**. 'Things' that some women grow into!

I think that critiquing a doer isn't doing. I think that we are so used to working hard that 'not working' is the new hard work. I think that a live broke man is luckier than a dead rich man. I think that **it will forever be now**. I think that a journey of a thousand lessons begins with a single misstep. I think that the internet killed community radio stations. I think that grown-ups who rant about how hard or unfair life is, will never grow up. I think that **sanity is overrated**. I am not fond of the word "normal" in its definition.

I think that saying that someone is full of themself is silly. Who else can one be full of except self? I think that a grown-up is merely an indoctrinated version of a kid. I think that commitment is slavery. I think that **the most quoted person is "Unknown."** I think that complaining about how freezing winter was, is a foolish way to spend a summer day. I think that everywhere is somewhere's somewhere. So, going "nowhere" is not doable. I think that being ashamed of how one looks must be hard. Seeing that one has to take one wherever one goes. I think that **love songs are nothing without exaggeration**. I think that life isn't really short. There are just too many good books to read in one lifetime. I think that grown-ups are aged kids. I think that celebrities are nothing without nobodies, yet they treat nobodies as nothing. I think that **to**

change the world, one has to ignore its residents. I think that an employment contract is the number one killer of dreams. I think that nobody is really proud to live in a township. People who claim to be are merely not ashamed of living there. I think that **making sense after-hours is overrated**. I think that gazillions of people design, but only a handful communicate. I think that not every-body will buy what you say, no matter how remarkable the said is. Some people are broke, intellectually. I think that the experienced maintain the status quo; while the naive change the world. I think that **committees kill unconventional ideas for a living**.

I think that a condom is probably the only "rubber" that avoids a mistake, as opposed to undoing the mistake. I think that if dead people knew how much good people will say about them at their funeral. Most would've faked their death beforehand. I think that the **fear of failure is a liability**. I think that complaining isn't really a deed. I think that not all whites are racists, and, not all racists are white. I think that a good head (intelligence, not hair style) makes good-looking women look good. I think that **courage is profitable**. I think that sanity is temporary. When turned on, we're all insane.

I think that prophecy kills perseverance. I think that man is today, an end product of what he did, and what he didn't do, yesterday. I think that **when a joker dies, the joke remains**. I think that weekends are life's gift to people who hate their jobs. I think that, thanks to the morgue, even boring people are 'cool' when they're buried. I think that **self-employment killed the weekend**. I think that an opinion that isn't read or heard is as good as unsaid. I think that speaking about interesting people does not necessarily make the speaker interesting. I think that life demands more "thinking" than "remembering." I think that **not trying is the new failure**.

I think that **to a zulu, every phone is an "iPhone."** I think that employment is slavery. Workers merely have a choice over where to serve their daily eight-hour sentence. I think that **being shy is a symptom of a low self-esteem**. I think that dating a wo/man with a kid is the new adoption. I think that by working very hard on Tuesday, to better your Wednesday, you are practically writing Thursday's history. I think that **friends are "family members" we have a "choice" over**. I think that "failures" are underrated.

I think that public opinion is to unconventional ideas; what abortion is to sperm. I think that **hard work is the new luck**. I think that exclusivity is paying more for less people to have what you're about to have. I think that love happens, it isn't proposed. I think that **hate hurts**. I think that gym is where big people who want to be smaller and small people who want to be bigger gather. I think that if society didn't honour fitting in, trends would be untrendy. I think that **being an artist is an art**. I think that the boring thing about loving one's work is that you find not working boring. I think that the lover in one's lover is not the most that one can uncover.

I think that the boring thing with 'No sex before marriage' is that kids will never get to attend their parents' wedding. I think that **unprotected sex is the new lottery.** I think that to have an open mind is to be intelligent. I think that a doer's deed creates employment for critics. I think that procrastination threatens critics' livelihood. I think that when a famous person mentions how he knows himself, that too counts as name-dropping. I think that an agnostic is a very low self-esteem having person that has 5 atheists and 5 Christian friends. I think that **bad design is bad.** We can't all be DJs. Someone has to do the dancing. I think that **debt is slavery.**

I think that with every second that your mouth is open, you lose an opportunity to learn from those that you're talking to. I think that **being is easy, being remarkable is hard.** I think that not all that is unknown does not exist. I think that talking about your plan to do something, isn't doing that thing. I think that on the other side of a 'rough patch' lies a wiser you. I think that **I am not my opinions.** I think that the prevalence of CDs must have had a negative impact on companies that sell pens. Seeing that most people used pens to "rewind" cassettes. I think that **death is too long.**

I think that intelligence is being ignorant enough to dream unrealistic dreams, foolish enough to work hard, and, too idiotic to give up. I think that **reality is what people who lack vision see.** I think that school fools a lot of people. Professionally, one thing isn't the most that one person can be. I think that if actions really speaks louder than words, then we should have had motivational doers, not motivational speakers. I think that **retro is a symptom of a generation that is too lazy to innovate.** I think that I think.

If People = Puppets, then Curiosity = Strings

I went to watch a 'hundred-and-eighty-four-minutes-long' movie, one boring Monday afternoon. Although the movie was intriguing, we all wished that the movie could just "... get to the point."

We passed the one-hour mark. And then the second-hour mark.

... with less than fifteen minutes left before "the end" of the film; a "technical error" happens — and then, the screen goes blank.

As one would expect, people started "moaning." At last, they demanded a refund. Either that, or for the movie "to be continued."

After a minute or six, the cinema's "representative" came in. And she then gave us an ultimatum: "... We'd like to apologize for the 'technical error.' We will replay the movie; but unfortunately, we cannot fast-forward to the part were the movie was before we experienced the technical glitch. So, it's either you come with me to get a refund, or you watch the film again, from the beginning."

Even though 'everybody' in there was already irritated by how long the movie took to get to the point; and then, there was the malfunction — we all chose to stay. All a hundred-and-ten plus of us!

If there is one thing that people hate, it's "not knowing." The fact that our prediction of how the movie will end won't be proved to be right or wrong, is the sole reason why we decided not to leave.

In a word, if you can invoke 'curiosity' in a person, you can control what he does or what he doesn't do next with ease. Curiosity is to people, what strings are to a puppet. Please, do pull with caution.

(Richard Whately phrased it brilliantly when he said that, "Curiosity is as much the parent of attention, as attention is of memory.")

Vocalists Are Dictators

I love music of all sorts; particularly jazz. The one thing that I like about instrumental songs is that such songs rarely dictate the listener's mood, and more importantly, .. what the listener thinks of.

All that you hear is the smooth sound of a trumpet. And, that's it! ... What, or who, one thinks of is usually the choice of the listener.

But do you think that it is possible not to think of your ex-lover when listening to The Manhattan's *"Kiss and Say Goodbye"*?

(Listen to that song, and, if you succeed in NOT thinking of a lover that you had to let go: it's either the volume was way too low; you need English lessons — or you have never had to let go of a lover.)

To Achieve More, Tell More Jokes

To achieve bigger dreams; dreams which "everybody" thinks of as stupid, "impossible," or, unrealistic; tell as many jokes as you can.

Although most do not realize it; people who frequently tell jokes, particularly jokes that they "came up with," the never tried-and-tested, are blessed with two precious attitudes. Not fearing failure (people not laughing at their joke) and not being concerned with what people will think of them, should their joke be funny or not.

Comedians are arguably the most frequent "failures," esp. during the early days of their careers. It takes guts to tell a joke to strangers. People who don't really owe you a laugh. What is worse is that they paid their hard-earned money, hence, they 'demand' a laugh.

Humour is the New Sex

As the world gets more and more 'clutter and noise' from marketers and advertisers; it inevitably gets harder by the minute, to get products to be "noticed," let alone to move products off the shelf.

As a result, advertising agencies find refuge in playing comedians.

An ad is aired. It is either funny or silly. Either way, it makes people laugh. People talk about the ad. The advertiser takes that as a sign of victory. But it rarely is. Awards get awarded. And, the creatives' egos triples. But the advertiser's bottom line doesn't. The message that the advert was intended to convey is 'suffocated' by the joke.

More often than not, the product loses the spotlight to the joke.

Inevitably, people have gotten accustomed to judging the merit of an ad based on how funny the ad is; and rarely on how appealing, "must-have," and, irresistible — has the ad made the advertised.

But ... I doubt that people make their final buying decisions based on who made them laugh the most or the longest. Alas, advertisers, patrons of such jokes, are blinded by the consumers' laughter.

Going are the days where unclothed wo/men are used to sell.

(Watch out Chris Rock, David Kau, Steve Harvey, Loyiso Gola, Dave Chappelle, Barry Hilton, Tumi Morake, et al., advertising agencies are trying to play the part that you so brilliantly play in our lives.)

The Song Must Outlive the Singer

I feel blessed to find fulfillment in doing work that makes a difference in people's days. And, at times, a difference in people's lives.

It is unfortunate that, in our times of modern slavery, the world is overpopulated with people who work solely to "... pay the bills."

And, as a result, only a handful demand work that is meaningful.

But, question is, if all that you do is, say, design 'flyers' for once-off events; how valuable will your art be, say, an hour after the event? And what difference will your art make, a day after your loved ones have placed a six-feet-divide of soil between you and the living?

How sad is it for a person that has worked for forty years to have nothing to show (except a golden watch and things that their job allowed them to buy on credit) for their forty years of hard work?

Out of the gazillions of things in the world ... which, and how many of them, would have not existed, should you have not existed?

Making art, work that makes a difference in people's lives, is arguably the only way that a person's work will "continue" to make a difference; even when that person is no longer amongst the living.

Alexander Bell might be late; but the telephone continues to ring.

When Leonardo da Vinci died, the *Mona Lisa* didn't. And, Miriam "Mama Afrika" Makeba is no more, yet, *A luta continua* continues to make a difference in people's lives. Enoch Sontonga too is late, however, *Nkosi Sikelel' iAfrika* continues to unite South Africans.

(Before starting to work on something, develop a 'habit' of asking yourself, "For how long will the about to be worked on matter?")

A Means to
an End

A car is not that important; Point B, the destination, is.

A movie theater is not that important; the movie is.

A wedding invitation is not that important; the wedding is.

A website is not that important; the "information" is.

Sex is not that important; the child is.

A microphone is not that important; the song is.

An unsuccessful attempt is not that important; the lesson is.

A book is not that important; the knowledge is.

Paint is not that important; the painting is.

A camera is not that important; the photograph is.

A farm is not that important; the potatoes are.

A joke is not that important; the laughter is.

A condom is not that important; the peace of mind is.

Crying is not that important; the healing is.

A logo is not that important; the brand it brings to mind is.

A lover letter is not that important; the confession is.

Viagra is not that important; the erection is.

"Whenever you find yourself on the side of the majority, it is time to pause and reflect."

— Mark Twain

The Past is Overrated

Yesterday might have dictated what one is, and what one has, today. But it doesn't have to dictate what one will be, and what one will have, tomorrow. It all depends on one's deeds (or lack thereof).

Remember that yesterday was tomorrow the day before yesterday.

... Which means that, by working very hard on Tuesday, to better your Wednesday, you are practically "writing" Thursday's history.

Needles to say, the irony is that, who, or what, you will be tomorrow, is dependent on what you do, or do not do, today. But when that 'tomorrow' comes, today, tomorrow's yesterday, won't matter.

(One of the reasons why we are 'victims' of the past is that we use the past as the basis of our identity. Fail on Monday, and, you are likely to still be seen, labeled, and, regarded as a failure, on Friday.)

Eight-Hour Shifts Are Overrated

An 8-hour shift breeds an illusion of productivity. Who the hell decided that 8 hours is the "most efficient" length of a shift that an employer can squeeze the most productivity out of an employee?

Which scenario is more profitable? An employee that brainstorms for an hour, contributes a remarkable idea, and then calls it a day. Or, an employee that, for the most part, plays solitaire to kill time;

her 8-hour sentence; who then, contributes a second-rate idea?

If employees are employed to 'contribute' ideas, shouldn't they be remunerated based on their contributions; and not on the number of hours that they have been under their employer's watchful eye?

Generally, employees are only productive for way less than half of their daily "working hours." And, as if not working during hours that they are paid for, is not enough; they end up wasting costly resources such as paper, electricity, water, coffee, bandwidth et al.

('Forcing' employees to serve their daily eight-hour sentence is the epitome of confusing movement with progress. While the rocking chair might rock; he who is "rocking" isn't really going anywhere.)

Proaction vs. Reaction

No matter who you are, or what you have, things that you do not go out looking for, will find you. Particularly, "unpleasant" things.

Granted, we generally do not have control over what "tomorrow" will have in store for us. So, we can either sit and let things happen to us, or we can involve ourselves in the process of making things happen. By doing something today to "influence" our tomorrow.

People who "sit and watch" things happen to them, rarely blame themselves. Life, other people, and, God top their scapegoats list.

If you really do not want to wet your hair — be "proactive" — by staying indoors, or by simply buying an umbrella; to avoid blaming Mother Nature for the rain that farmers need to keep us well-fed.

(... to avoid "blaming" a condom for breaking; abstain from sex.)

Opinions of the Rest of the World

At the core of most people's fear of failure, lies one of the world's silliest questions, "... What will 'other people' say or think of me?"

Nonetheless, whether you are good or bad, underweight or over-weight, whether you do or do not; people will forever have something to say. So, why worry about them having something to say?

What 'other people' think of you is mostly dependant on nothing but how they think and how they perceive you. Like "Unknown" said, "What 'other people' think of you is none of your business."

(It is rare to find a doer, an achiever, that spends her time talking about things that others have said or done. More often than not, it is only people who have nothing to 'bless the world' with that do.)

Being Right is Overrated

Being right, the longing of every "sensible" arguer, is overrated.

The thing is that whenever you prove or realize that you are right; the only thing that you will get is the confirmation that you know what you know and the fact that what you know is indeed 'right.'

(... Now enters the greatest tutor of them all. Being "wrong.")

When you are wrong, to most, you are a 'temporary failure.' But I beg to differ. I assert that failure is nothing but a blessing; a brick that is of vital importance in building one's "mansion of wisdom."

The frequency of your being wrong will determine how much new knowledge you will acquire. So, when in an argument, pray to be the 'wrong' one. And, be wrong as frequently as you possibly can.

You will get to take home a lesson; while he who is right, is left.

(... Left with nothing but a consolation price; an ego stroke.)

Those Who Think Daily, Should Be Paid Daily

Creatives and thinkers don't solve the same challenges day in, day out. Not by a long shot. So, why should they earn a fixed income?

I think that it is only fair to be paid based on the value of the ideas that one has contributed in a particular day, week, month, or project — not on the number of hours that one has spent in an office.

(But then again, what am I expecting, in our world overpopulated with people who find comfort in the "safety" of "secure" jobs?)

The Cycle of Freedom

A friend introduces an 'orthodox' man to an 'orthodox' woman.

... And, after a few months, weeks, days, or even hours, of promising each other "forever," the man and the woman have sex.

A few months later, usually nine, an unorthodox offspring springs.

The man and the woman then choose a name for the offspring.

And, as a matter of course, with the greatest obliviousness, and, subtlety, the man and the woman coerce their beliefs on their kid.

The kid has no choice over her name, and, on who to call God.

The kid then grows into an orthodox adult. Eventually, she meets an orthodox lover. After a few months, weeks, or days of promising each other forever — the offsprings bring an offspring to being.

It is only then that the man and the woman will have the freedom to choose a name and a belief. But the kids, now turned parents, will only have the freedom to choose for their kid, not themselves.

(To have the freedom to choose; their kid will have to have a kid.)

The Human Divide, by Difference

We, as human beings, are all members of the human race.

But, be that as it may, there are untold reasons (read: excuses) for John to see Sarah as "persona non grata." Unavoidably, prejudice, discrimination, and, hate are usually 'by-products' of such divides.

John is from Africa, and, Sarah is from Asia.

John is from South Africa, and, Sarah is from Nigeria.

John is from Gauteng, and, Sarah is from Limpopo.

John is from Soweto, and, Sarah is from Tembisa.

John is from Pimville, and, Sarah is from Dobsonville.

John is white, and, Sarah is black.

John is homosexual, and, Sarah is heterosexual.

John is Venda, and, Sarah is Xhosa.

John is into soccer, and, Sarah is into rugby.

John supports Orlando Pirates, and, Sarah supports Kaizer Chiefs.

John is wealthy, and, Sarah is poor.

John is underweight, and, Sarah is overweight.

John is a Christian, and, Sarah is a Muslim.

John likes Michael Jackson, and, Sarah likes Prince.

John is ancient, and, Sarah is wet behind the ears.

John likes Chris Rock, and, Sarah likes David Kau.

John likes Jazz, and, Sarah likes Rock.

John is an extrovert, and, Sarah is an introvert.

John is a giant, and, Sarah is a midget.

John is a vegetarian, and, Sarah loves steak.

~~John's blood is red, and, Sarah's blood is red.~~

(... And, the divide, by difference, continues ...)

"It's amazing that the amount of news that happens in the world every day always just exactly fits the newspaper."

— Jerry Seinfeld

Supply End Demand

In business, satisfying what the market demands is fairly simple.

An entrepreneur realizes that people who don't want to have kids, as yet, are busy having sex. The entrepreneur then sees a business opportunity in selling condoms to those with "habits like rabbits."

... It is that simple. Nothing wrong, or special, with that.

With that said, while consumer feedback is imperative to any business that's serious about survival; more often than not, it leads to a company that does nothing but help maintain "the status quo."

In most cases, customers only realize what they need, after you've given it to them. Like Henry Ford said, should he have asked people what they wanted; they would have demanded "faster horses."

Teamwork is Overrated

The larger the committee that an idea had to please before it was approved, the less 'unconventional' the idea is likely to have been.

That is to say, committees kill "unconventional" ideas for a living.

It is "impossible" to convince dozens of people to buy into a never done, seen, or heard of, idea. There'd be too many varying 'tastes' that the idea will have to appeal to. And varying levels of courage.

The most efficient teams are those made of individuals who take charge of their own unique tasks. Otherwise, the project will take longer than necessary to be approved, shipped, or, launched.

Furthermore, such arrangements give incompetent team members an opportunity to hide behind the bunch. That's bad news for both the employer and the incompetent employees (it will be impractical to better, or build on, a flaw that is "concealed"). And, ... that is also unfair to the remaining diligent competent "team players."

Although teamwork is the best arrangement to "disperse" blame whenever something goes wrong — it is not the best organization for individuals to flourish, esp. the "incompetent" team members.

In a partnership of two: if one partner can 'effortlessly' replace the other; then the other partner is unnecessary. A partnership is only profitable when it is a synthesis of varying skills, expertise, talents, and, insights. As well as, the sharing of varying responsibilities by the partners — not a "mimicking" of each other's know-how.

For a burger to be. The person that makes patties should pair with one that makes buns — not with another that too makes patties.

(Rather have twelve "different" colours aiming to form a rainbow, rather than a hundred shades of purple trying to form a rainbow.)

Strange Strangers

I'm fond of strangers who smile at people that they do not know.

The most painless (like all puns in this book, this pun too is intended) way to kill a stranger is by 'introducing' yourself. All it takes is a, "Hi, I'm (enter your name)." ... to eternally get rid of a stranger.

Why I Rarely Do "Client Work"

I truly love the challenges that some projects present to the graphic designer in me. All that I aspire to produce is; the 'most' efficient visual communication solution that will help my clients meet their marketing or branding objectives. But, unfortunately, the most efficient design, and, what clients usually dictate, are seldom one.

Firstly, I design, and, "think design," every single day. And, I have been doing so for the past seven years or so. Yet, clients, most of whom are 'thinking design' for the first time in their lives, have the final say as to which design solution gets to see the light of day.

Typically, a client's "choice" is based on their personal tastes; even though their business and them aren't one. Green, pink, and, yellow — Susan Brown's favourite colours — are not necessarily the best colour scheme for Susan Brown's Bakery's corporate identity.

So, inevitably, most designers spend most of their time defending a design solution, or, a fitting colour that the client passionately hates. Merely because the colour is the client's ex-lover's favourite.

"...My ex-Boo loves blue too. So, blue is also out of the question."

Alternatively, I could play puppet; a being with "no brain" but fluency in a design software. Give such clients "whatever" that they demand, and, just be thankful that I will be able to pay rent that month. But life is way 'too short' to settle for "not-that-bad" type of work — all in the name of keeping one's landlord's mouth shut.

For such reasons, I only work with clients who are comfortable in giving me a "Doctor and Patient" relationship, respect, and, carte blanche. Only a few are brave enough to do so. Through merging my expertise, and, their insights, we create work that yields great returns for their brands. Not work that merely boosts their egos.

Secondly, I have decided to spend 'almost all' of my time, and, energy, doing work that makes a difference to humanity; regardless of how small the impact of my work might have on the human race.

... In some cases, I manage to change perceptions. In other cases, I make people "question" the status quo, and, at times, I inspire.

So, if I manage to provoke a dreamer's thought and that dreamer ends up making a difference to the human race; partly due to the impact that my art had on her. Then my art has contributed to that difference. But she can, by all means, take all the credit. Because credit is given to he who did — not he who inspired the doer to do.

To me, art is any kind of work that "touches" everybody that it is exposed to. And, that also includes people who have not paid the creator of such work — people who do not really "own" the art.

For example, I publish visual poetry (*via* ah-damn-and-if.com). And for the "lifespan" of the T-shirt: any person that buys a tee is likely to spread the message (on the T-shirt) to hundreds, if not, thousands of people. So, one person pays for the tee and hundreds or thousands of people are afforded the opportunity to extract value out of the visual poem; without having to pay even a cent. Bingo!

Fine, you've designed a "cool poster" for a client. It helped them lure more people to their event. They paid you. They've seen a return on the money they've invested in the poster. And then what?

(What difference did that 'transaction' make to the human race?)

Dress Codes Are Overrated

All that one owes the rest of the world is to not "show up" naked.

When Better Doesn't Matter

How would candles 'work' and what would they look like; should companies that make candles, try to compete with light bulbs; an 'invention' that, without a doubt, immensely shrank their profits?

In there lies one of the many "positive" facets of competition.

But to make the most of that, one must look for the things that makes them unique and extraordinary; not cheap tactics to "kill" one's competitors, or, to fight newer technology.

Light bulbs, though "better than" candles, can never give one a candle lit dinner. As a matter of fact, a candle lit dinner would not be so "romantic," should light bulbs have not been.

The f.Law of Law

Once traffic lights give way to pedestrians; cars coming from the other direction are 'supposed to' stop. But one might not. And, as a result, some undertaker might have to undertake a burial.

The person next to you (friend, foe, or, stranger) isn't supposed to kill you. But she might make the last time that you saw your loved ones — the last time. In such instances, "assumption" is deadly.

Laws don't prevent unlawfulness, they just encourage obedience.

Luxury is Nothing Without the Poor

What is the use of buying a watch worth twelve million dollars; if the people around you will not be aware of the price tag? I mean, cheap watches too will read "Eight o'clock" — come Eight o'clock — wouldn't they? I stand to be corrected. But I think they too will.

... So, it will be Eight o'clock at Eight o'clock. Whether you are in a mansion, or, in a shack. Whether you are in a taxi, or, in a Ferrari.

Even though "almost all" people who do are likely to argue otherwise; people rarely buy expensive things without entertaining the thought of what "others" will think of them, or, say about them.

That is called "conspicuous consumption." The lavish spending on goods and services; mainly for the purpose of displaying one's income, or, one's wealth. Such display serves as a conspicuous consumer's means of attaining, or, maintaining their social status.

It is the fact that such-and-such area's right of admission is limited, or reserved, that makes "very important people," very important. What would a VIP area be without the not-so-important people?

(I mean, what would a "Limited Edition" be without the "limit"?)

"It Sounds Like a Cliché, But ... "

The forever overused phrase, "... this may sound like a cliché, but ..." is starting to be itself. Talk about the kettle calling pot black!

"The worst part about politics is that you're always right and no one ever knows it."

— Unknown

Homosexuals Too
Have Armpits

When I see a homosexual person; I either see a brother, or, a sister. At times, some are so 'dramatic' that one can't help but see both.

Anyways, even though I'm of the sexual orientation that the Bible endorses in the Book of Genesis; I respect every single member of the human race. Whether they're turned on by a bra, or, by a bro.

The Molestation of Consumers

Instead of selling the typical "scientific fact" that a deodorant will eliminate body odour; marketers are likely to subtly sell something that almost everybody would trade their souls to have. Sex appeal.

But is it fair for marketers to 'exploit' our desire to be sexually appealing? Come on, it is marketers we are talking about! The same people who are notorious for making tap water appear uncool in the eyes of the "glass holder." All in the name of "bottled water."

When growing up, we had one type and brand of moisturizer that we willingly shared as a family. Fast forward to today. But these days there's this-and-that for women and this-and-that for men. It could be that men and women's skin really demand different things from a lotion. Or that marketers succeeded in fooling us — again.

Back to Marketing and Sexual Orientation

If marketers are to effectively take advantage of people's desire to be sexually appealing; shouldn't there be advertisements where, say, a man sprays himself with this-and-that by brand so-and-so, goes somewhere, and then, leave other men "drooling" over him?

(... the same could obviously be done when selling to "lesbians.")

Could it be because brands do not want to risk having the stigma that 'some' heterosexuals, arguably the majority, have attached to homosexuality? Will such ads make brands and/or their products "homo" — or, at best, "mark" them with such a "dirty" name?

How effective is an ad that shows a man using a deodorant which ultimately leads to women finding him impossible to resist — to a man that is attracted to other men? Is the "population" of homosexuals too minuscule to justify a marketer's consideration?

(Er, ... I don't know about you; but I've never seen a penniless gay.)

I think that acknowledging gays and lesbians in our marketing efforts has an enormous power to "educate" our ignorant brothers and sisters who are busy killing their own brothers and sisters — merely because they have a 'sexual preference' different to theirs.

That there is what every social entrepreneur longs for. An opportunity to build wealth and financial freedom for self and the generation to follow; while making a 'positive contribution' to humanity.

(Again, ... I await an eccentric brand with sufficient supply of guts.)

The Ironic Thing About Sport

I think that sport is arguably the only thing in the world that manages to unite people by dividing them. Sport divides us to unite us.

So maybe, just maybe, governments should spend more of taxpayers' money on balls, bats, wickets, swimming pools, whistles, grass, goal posts, sand, racing tracks et al., and less on nuclear weapons.

(That would make stadiums and racetracks the new "battlefield.")

Plan B's Kill Plan A's

Having a Plan B is a hint that one does not believe in their Plan A. But, why waste your time and energy on Plan A in the first place?

That's comparable to running a marathon with money for a cab in your hand. Just incase you get too lazy to continue with the race.

Actor, Will Smith, famously said that, "There's no reason to have a Plan B, because it distracts from Plan A." I think that's wisely said!

As it happens, nobody has ever changed the world with a Plan B. Windows wasn't Bill Gate's Plan B. Music was not Sipho Gumede's Plan B. Golf isn't Tiger Woods' Plan B. Acting isn't John Kani's Plan B. Football wasn't Pelé's Plan B. Writing isn't Maya Angelou's Plan B. In addition, independence was not Mahatma Gandhi's Plan B.

Photoshop™ Killed Reality

People are now so conscious of "photo manipulation," that even 'genuine' photographs are considered to be manipulated. Should the beholder not believe or like what they see in the photograph.

Automatically, as a result, a 'photographed' adulterer that has just been caught (or rather: shot) with his pants down; can confidently and forcefully argue about how 'manipulated' the photographs is.

(Oh, ... Photoshop™ also killed the saying, "Seeing is believing.")

SOMETHING % OFF

Generally, a sale is a sign of customers having bought ten pairs of trousers, from a retailer that bought a hundred from a wholesaler.

Offering a 'sale' is a quick profit-seeking tactic that creates a conflict between the brand manager and the brand's sales department.

From a salesperson's point of view, offering a "clearance sale" is a logical means to up the business's sales. Plus, that also makes the reaching of their "sales targets" a little bit easier. While, on the other hand, offering endless clearance sales is harmful to the business — when looking at it from the brand manager's standpoint.

A stockist that sells different brands does not really care about the long-term brand image of the brands that he sells; like the brand owners do. All he thinks of, is a way to make as much money as possible — from the brand equities that the brands currently enjoy.

Equities that took the brand owners millions and eons to build.

Granted, a sale is likely to lure more customers, and better still, attract customers who wouldn't afford the brand sans the discount.

But that inevitably leaves the brand's loyal patrons feeling cheated.

They pay ninety-six dollars for a product, and then, say, two weeks later, the stockist sells the very same product for thirty-five dollars.

What's worse is that, frequently offering a sale trains customers to wait for sales. Which means that unless there's a sale, even people who afford to buy, will wait for the next "clearance sale" to buy.

(A 'sale' also suggests that the product was sort of "overpriced.")

Children vs. "Grown-ups"

Children are the most ambitions "creatures" of us all. Alas, that is until some childish "grown-up" teaches them to "... be realistic."

Grown-ups bully kids into believing the limits that they were fed by "grown-ups," when they too were kids; on kids who care to listen.

(In short, a grown-up is merely an 'indoctrinated' version of a kid.)

The Thing with Critics

Some artists aren't "painting" because they have run out of paint, and, at times, a blank canvas. Some are merely lazy, and, the rest are scared of what "critics" will say about them and/or their work.

(Sadly, ... the irony is that, without a doer, a critic is "useless.")

So, the same people who give sense to a critic's being are terrified of critics. Talk about an employer that is scared of her employee!

The only deed that a critic does, is "talking" about a doer's deed, the done. I mean, what's a soccer commentator without a soccer match? Nothing but noise. Moreover, critiquing a doer isn't doing.

Every time a doer does, a critic is blessed with a job opportunity.

In a nutshell, a doer is to a critic, what a company looking for an employee, is to an unemployed suitable candidate.

By writing this book, I did. Therefore, by that very act, I have sort of created employment for a few critics out there who would have kept their month shut — should this book have not been written.

(Go ahead, "critic" this writing. Tell every single person that cares enough to listen — about what you think of what I think of you.)

I Pray Not to Fall for an Actress

I doubt that I'd date an actress. Not that there's anything "wrong" with "them." I just don't think that I have the "wisdom" to do so.

The thought of my woman, my better half, being 'licked' by some random man, all in the name of entertaining the rest of the world, is way too much for someone with no wisdom like me to handle.

I know that I would be "expected" to take that the same way as watching a cook cook. But then, what is reality? Are 'real people' allowed to fictionalize reality; while fiction can not realize reality?

... When a woman kisses another woman's husband behind closed doors; it is called "cheating." Yet, should the very same man and woman kiss in front of a camera man — "acting" it will be called.

Is cheating dependent on who else is aware of the "smooching"?

(So, one's other half can do 'whatever' they please, with another's lover, so long as they know that the other half's other half knows that they know that he, or she, knows? ... things we do for rent!)

"A man's face is his autobiography.
A woman's face is her work of fiction."

— Oscar Wilde

The Anatomy of a Creative's Bill

The one thing that a minimalist and a creative have in common, is that their work is "simpler" than the number of zeros on their bill.

Granted, almost every single person that has "access" to a design software, can replicate Nike, Apple, or, Neotel's logo. And, as one would expect, that generally leads to whoever that hired the creative — or the minimalist — wondering where their money went.

However, it is the creatives' coming up with such remarkable ideas behind such logos, that makes every "expensive" creative, expensive. Not the complexity of their design, or, how difficult it was to bring their idea to being. Bringing ideas to being is relatively easy.

We all knew of the words: "Just", "do", and, "it." But not all of us, if any at all, would have came up with "Just do it." Should we have been commissioned to coin a slogan for Nike's ad campaign.

A perfect example, would be of an architect. She is paid to come up with design solutions for buildings; while those that she usually supervises, those who do the "actual" building, are paid peanuts when compared to what the architect will earn. And, the reason?

... Simple. While it sure requires skills to do the actual building of a building; every single builder is replaceable with ease. And that's highly because builders do not really create. They merely follow orders — the design, the map, the plan, the blueprint, the prototype.

So, the lion's share of a web designer's bill is made of their coming up with an "effectual" user interface; not coding as per the user interface mock-up, per se. That is the easy part. Eons can do that.

(He who 'writes' a play earns more than those who play the play.)

Don't Judge Kids with Kids

Never ever judge a kid, simply because she has a kid. For that kid that you're comparing her to, might have had an abortion. Twice.

That certainly makes one think differently about "What You See Is What You Get." A phrase that most people use to describe themselves (under: biography) on websites like Facebook, and, the like.

(Generally, what one gets, is what one cannot, or did not, "see.")

Employee of the Month

A reward and award too 'ridiculous' for my liking. Seeing that, the best that a secretary can be, is an A1 secretary. So, why make her compete for the "Employee of the Month" title with the tea lady?

Besides, even if a company has two secretaries; the two are there to work, and maybe collaborate, not to compete against each other.

When employees are given an opportunity to do work that matters to them — work that they genuinely love doing — they do the best that they can. So, pushing employees to "compete" to have their portrait "paraded" on the company's wall is a silly "incentive" to try to get the most possible productivity out of such employees.

(Rather give them responsibilities that builds and challenges them. Instead of a temporary 'title' that they fight for; every four weeks.)

Don't Judge Prostitutes

Like I asserted earlier, where there is an immense demand, supply will forever be. Ipso facto, should the need to be judgmental be, judge he who demands. Not she who is meeting the demand. In a word ... judge he who's pleased; not she who pleased the pleased.

... So, if you truly think that all-night parties are "disgusting," do judge those who dance to the music — not the poor disc jockeys.

(To end the life of an intruding tree; cut its roots, not its branches.)

Pleasing Google is Overrated

Which "porn star" doesn't want to be on top? On top of the first search engine results page (for all "porn star" queries) on Google.

As idea merchants who primarily rely on the Internet to spread our ideas; we naturally become susceptible to any second-rate claims by any random person that promises to help us direct traffic our website's way. A lot of SEO (search engine optimization) "gurus" assert that content producers should publish new content at least once a day; to augment their chances of being found via Google.

The thing that makes a search engine query so powerful; is that it directs people who are in search for, say, secondhand teaspoons, to Sarah's Secondhand Teaspoons's website. Bingo! Relevance is a valuable thing. I mean, what's the use of reciting Genesis 1:1 to an atheist?

However, as an entrepreneur, if your business's survival (be it website traffic, or, new business) is 'solely' dependent on traffic from search engines; then your days as an entrepreneur are numbered.

I say, ... be remarkable. Offer a remarkable product or service. And, people will start talking about how remarkable you are. Inevitably, as a result, your poor company's bookkeeper will be kept busy.

If you love writing, please do so. But only 'publish' when you have something meaningful to say. Ask yourself this, "can the world do without this writing?" Whenever you answer "yes," don't publish.

I have a design journal, where I write about, well, "design." But I don't have a set "publishing frequency." I do not even brainstorm things that I will write about next. While most "bloggers" average two writings on their busy week; I am happy with four annually.

Below is an extract from an email that I have recently received from a reader of my design journal. A design "student" from Portugal:

> "... I am writing you to let you know I like your writings a lot, and the fact that you don't try to post all that frequently, but that you wait to say something meaningful. Although I like your writings, and would obviously like to see more, I wouldn't trade more frequent posting for a loss of quality." — **Vítor Galvão**

Granted, search engine optimization is "important." But I doubt it had anything to do with the successes of the iPod and the iPhone.

People befriend "like-minded" people. So, if you write remarkable writings about, say, design; Neo is likely to tell Lerato about your writings. Since he is "certain" that they will add value to her too.

(In a word, an entrepreneur whose business solely relies on search engines to bring in business; will very soon be in need of his CV.)

The Lifespan of a Title

Is he still a writer, because a book he once wrote? And, is she still a biker, because a bike she once rode? If this writing was to be my last writing; would I still be a writer tomorrow? If the last ride that she had, was to be her last; would she 'still be' a biker tomorrow?

It has been over 6 weeks since I designed something. Question is, am I still a graphic designer today? In a word, am I what I am, because of what I'm currently doing or because of what I have done?

Education Doesn't Breed Sense

When you have something to say; what matters to me is whatever that you have to say. Not you, your past, the school that you went to, or the exams that you passed a decade ago. Add to that whatever that your 'former bosses' used to call you (previous job titles).

My agreeing or disagreeing with, and, my liking or hating of, what you have to say, has nothing to do with the universities you went to, the years it took you to earn your qualification, or the fact that you were the "first black prefect" in a school full of white people.

It's only after I have been wowed by your rants, thinking, writings, deeds, or insights, that I'm likely to ask, "... Who the hell is this?"

(It is only then that Google, your CV, or your URL, will be of value to me. Until then keep your grade 8 geography marks to yourself.)

"The conventional view serves to protect us from the painful job of thinking."

— John K. Galbraith

The Weight of a Gift

How much the recipient values a gift is dependent on two things:

1. How much value will the gift add, and, what difference will the gift make (to them, or, in their lives). And, more importantly, ...

2. How much of a sacrifice is the giver making in giving the given.

A twenty-six dollar donation from someone who had nothing but thirty dollars in his name; will be more valued than a ten-thousand dollar donation from a donor with a "twelve-digit" bank balance.

(That is to say, a patient is likely to value a 10-minute visit from an extremely busy friend; more than an 8-hour visit from a friend that is visiting merely because he had nothing to do or nowhere to go.)

Growth is the Birth of Death

... And, at the very same time, growth is the death of birth.

The advancement of technology afforded *Google*, *Digg*, *Amazon*, *Kalahari.net*, *YouTube*, *Flickr*, *Afrigator*, *WordPress*, *Twitter*, *75*, *Facebook*, *Zappos*, *eBay* and the like, an "opportunity" to be.

However, because of the very same technological metamorphosis; businesses that sell correction fluids to keep their landlord's mouth shut (brands like Tipp-Ex™ and Wite-Out™) are 'close to' being declared "dead", "pointless", "useless", or, "prehistoric."

(So, a farmer and a homeless person are unlikely to welcome rain with the same amount of enthusiasm and gratitude. When a husband dies, the wife loses a lover — the undertaker gains a client.)

Rappers Don't Age Well

Imagine, if you will, your father wearing an oversized pair of pants and a doo-rag. ~~Singing~~ Mumbling his lungs out — Jumping up and down for kids way younger than you — Kids who paid him to entertain them — with a groupie or seven screaming his name.

There is nothing strange with a kid entertaining kids to pay rent.

... It is only when the kid, the one who does the entertaining, gets "older," while the kid's "clients" remains five- to twelve-year-olds.

If pleasing kids is at the core of your paying rent; then you are no different from a soccer player. The life span of your "coolness" is momentary. Your patrons matures, while you don't. Well, sort of.

On the other hand, it is completely different with business and entrepreneurship. Seeing that even a sixty-year-old entrepreneur can exist solely to serve, or please, six-year-olds without looking "silly."

The moral of the story? Have the end in mind, before you start. At times, time kills relevance. Not everything should be done forever.

(... A great example would be the phases of a "typical" criminal. While he's still young, fast, and, agile; he snatch purses. But as he gets older and slower — he puts food on the table by doing crimes that requires less, or preferably no, "speed", or, physical strength.)

How Original Are Original Writings?

To a certain extent, ... readers are fed knowledge that their feeder was fed by a feeder — "who too" — was fed by another feeder.

"Almost" every single writing written on a particular subject, say, branding, is made of either an opinion, or, a fact. Anyhow, both facts and opinions are subject to one's knowledge or lack thereof.

We were born with minds void of knowledge, thus, the little that we know; we found. So, are we, as people, entitled to ownership of our knowledge, or, accreditation to our opinions; even though, almost everything that a man knows was taught by another man?

... Briefly, when I share an opinion, do I really "own" that opinion?

(There surely was a time where a writer couldn't count up to one.)

Writers Are So Overrated

Wisdom isn't knowing everything; it starts with knowing that you don't know everything. I'd like to invite you to share your wisdom. So, ... in the following 10 pages I'll keep my ~~mouth~~ keyboard shut to afford you an opportunity to share your ideas and wisdom.

On the surface, this seems insignificant. But think of all the people whose hands this book will end up in. Your writings could change their day — or their lives. [No copy of this book will be 'identical.']

Please don't forget to write your name at the end of your writings. I think you deserve to be credited for your ideas and wisdom. By the way, you don't have to fill all blank lines. You can write a few lines; log your name; and then give whoever that will get to read this copy someday, an opportunity to also share their rants, ideas, or, wisdom.

"Knowledge grows when shared."

— Bhartrihari

Be "Childish" for as Long as You Can

Naiveté is one of the most "valuable," and, underestimated things that human beings are blessed with, when they are born. And, by that very fact, children rarely entertain the thought of something being impossible. Furthermore, because of that, every single child "wholeheartedly" believes that they can fly, or, change the world.

I honestly believe that they can. They just don't want to show off.

... Alas, that is until society pollutes their precious minds with poisonous words like "impossible" and phrases like "... be realistic!"

Do the world a favour. Be childish, be unrealistic. Believe in things not yet done or seen. Naiveté is a trait that those who had the guts to change the world; as a result, leave a "dent," have in common.

It is either you are naïve, or, you are maintaining the status quo.

(Whenever what you do, or don't do, is considered to be a sign of "maturity," chances are that you are finding comfort and safety in deeds already done, or, in dreams already dreamt. Proven "stuff.")

People Who Wear G-Strings Suffer from Indecision

Er, ... I know that it is foolish to judge a road that you have never travelled, or, a deed that you have never done. But, I think that G-strings are one of the worst inventions ever. And that people who wear G-strings should make their minds up. It is either they cover their assets, or, they don't. So, they should stop trying to do both.

... One cannot be "draked." Dressed and naked at the same time.

(But then again, that will highly depend on the wearers' definition of naked. And that of dressed. In other words, which parts needs to be "covered" ... before "nudity" can be declared "no more.")

Stop Shouting: Those People are Deaf!

Relevance is arguably the most important thing in communication.

Not every sportsperson will value, or, "give a damn" about what Nike stands for. For that reason; no amount of discounts, advertising, or spam, will convert such people into enthusiastic Nike fans.

... Not every person that can be spoken to, should be spoken to.

(No amount of brilliant creative writing or cool graphic design can stimulate a burning desire to own a Koran, in a diehard Christian.)

The Medium and the Small-minded

"Small-minded" producers are 'largely' fooled by their "medium."

A "prostitute" sells orgasms; not her "lips and hips."

A "restaurateur" sells food; not "plates and cutlery."

A "school" sells education; not "textbooks and homework."

A "book publisher" sells writings; not "ink and paper."

As convention gets tattooed in the minds of some producers, they forget what it is that they're actually selling. As a result, we now have record labels that use the time that they could be making more music with, to defend Compact Discs. And, book publishers who could be publishing more writings are busy defending paper.

(A record label sells music; not round plastics ... with round holes.)

The Irony of Unpredictability

Generally, people find "new" things "interesting" ... they get used to them, and then, they get bored. And, eventually, predictability makes things that were 'initially' regarded as "interesting" boring.

That then makes unpredictability interesting to those who wish to remain interesting. But, be that as it may, the very same people who are fascinated by one's unpredictability will before long adopt a habit of successfully predicting that one will be unpredictable. Which will automatically make one's unpredictability predictable.

In a case where one has successfully 'surprised' people a hundred and ninety-nine times — wouldn't those people's being surprised by one's two hundredth deed, to some extent, be "unsurprising"?

(To be perpetually inconsistent is to be 'consistently' inconsistent.)

Being Talked About is the New Advertising

Almost all 'remarkable' brands in the world do not "advertise." It is either that, or they do very little advertising. Mostly to introduce new products. Even so, they are more profitable than brands that spend hundred times more on advertising that sell so-so products.

Having a remarkable product is the easiest hard way to advertise.

... with so much marketing noise around, the only way to stand a chance of thriving, is by being talked about. If people are not talking about your product; it is best that you start updating your CV.

Almost all of Google and Apple's advertising was, and is likely to remain, done by their avid fans. No money spent there. Just a few wowed people who inevitably told their friends about the two brands. The "loudest" ad won't necessarily yield the most returns.

A remarkable product is a profit-yielding marketing tool in itself.

(Things like book covers, brand names, book titles, logos, slogans, et al., affords even small broke brands an opportunity to be talked about. So, why spend millions on advertising, when you could let your, say, slogan, do the "talking," or the "being talked about"?)

A Billionaire Has Billionaires' Problems

If the lack of 'contentment' in your life is solely due to the lack of this-or-that, then contentment will "forever be" a pipe dream.

John might choose to see the "homelessness" in him. But I might choose to see a person free from the slavery that debt causes in most people's lives, in him. And, Sarah might be frustrated by the pedestrian in her. But I might choose to see a woman free from financial commitments (installments, petrol, insurance, etc.) in her.

"Not having" is not excuse enough to be "ungrateful." And, on top of that, having has its own demands and commitments which might, sooner or later, lead to excuses for being content no more.

(A billionaire that lives the life of a billionaire receives a billionaire's bill at the end of the month. That there is the beauty of relativity.)

The Curse of Instant Gratification

A human being is a creature that finds pleasure in getting things, which he wants to need, as quick and as easy as he possibly can.

Sadly, because of such a "weakness," instant gratification has inevitably led to a society where "the majority" would rather make sixty dollars a year today, than to be broke today, so that they will be able to make a hundred dollars a day, in, say, four years' time.

A salary is one of the world's most enslaving forms of instant gratification. A fix that employers fix employees with, every 4 weeks.

Who a person is, and what she has, is merely a reflection of how good, or bad, she has been with the art of delaying gratification.

(More often than not, the longest that a typical employee is willing, and, is able to, delay gratification for, is merely four weeks.)

"The three most harmful
addictions are heroin, carbohydrates,
and, a monthly salary.

— Nassim Nicholas Taleb

The Lifespan of Shock in Marketing

Attracting attention, and, being talked about, is getting harder by the minute. So, ... what is the most logical "shortcut" to realizing the two? Shock people! Well, that's what some marketers believe.

There was this white guy with a stage name of 'Lekgoa.' Which is a SeTswana word that translates into "a white person" in English.

... He was probably "the first white" kwaito (a music genre that emerged in South Africa) artist. If not, he was the first white artist to perform a kwaito song on Jam Alley (a music show). Anyhow ...

He had one of the most nonsensical lyrics that Kwaito has ever produced. But he was all over the place. CDs where moving. Rent was paid + a living was made. Papers even ran stories with head-lines like, *"White boy sings kwaito."* This was obviously shock-ing. Especially in a country where apartheid was. People were shocked, "Wow! A white man singing in a black man's lingo ...?"

Another "shocking" story. Still within South Africa. And kwaito.

(... this was way before Lekgoa uttered his first SeTswana word.)

There was this big guy (by weight, not fame) named Tsekeleke.

His gimmick? The 1st overweight person to sing about how fat he is. Somewhere in his songs are the words "... Fatty Boom Boom!"

And again, people were more "shocked" than amused. "Wow! A fat person publicly singing about how fat he is?!" While shock helped the two above mentioned artists put food on the table; there was no way that their "Unique selling propositions" could have remained profitable. There is no way that you can surprise people, repeatedly, with the very same thing. Even if you meet a 'scary' woman with seven eyes; you'll eventually get used to her.

People get used to things, and then, they get bored. That is probably why chivalry is short-lived. And why infidelity will forever be.

(In a word, "Breaking News" can, at its most, only "break" once.)

The Other Thing with Critics

… They must, until hell freezes over, have "something" to say.

That's to say, it is impossible for a critic to honestly have absolutely nothing to say. If the critic cannot find something to critic — he would rather look for something to "compliment" the doer on.

When a critic is asked to do what they do, critic, and he does not have anything to say, that makes him appear as if he is "clueless."

A critic is like a daily newspaper. Come tomorrow, they must have something to say. What that means is that, there'll never be a day where a newspaper has "no news" to feed its readers. And, in the very same way, there will never be a critic that has nothing to say.

So, … the likelihood of a critic replying with, "No comment …!" is equivalent to that of an atheist shouting, "… Praise the Lord!"

(Go ahead, critic this writing. And, as a result, prove me "right.")

A House is Rarely an Asset

Though a house has the potential to be an asset; most are not assets. A house is a liability until it's paid off. And even then, so long as the house does not bring in money, it will remain a "liability."

A house will only be an asset once its owner decides to rent it out.

(A true asset earns, not cost, you money. So, to increase the odds of your house turning into an asset — you have to "move out.")

The Majority vs. The Best

The majority of workers work for eight hours a day. But that's not necessarily the most efficient number of hours that an employer can enslave an employee with, in a day, in their pursuit to squeeze the "most effectiveness of productive effort" from the employee.

"The majority" of workers work for other people. But that is not necessarily the best way for one to make a living, to pay off one's debts, to change people's lives, or, to leave a "dent" in this world.

"The majority" of workers are only paid "every four weeks." Once a month. But that is not necessarily the best 'modus operandi' to realizing financial freedom or keeping one's landlord's mouth shut.

"The majority" of employers rely on a CV (the past) to judge a job seeker. But that's not necessarily the best way to "predict" the potential (the future) of a job seeker.

"The majority" of Christians name their kids after "characters" in the Bible. But that's not necessarily the best names to name a kid.

"The majority" of employees are mostly happy on paydays. But that's not necessarily the "best days" to put a smile on one's face.

Generally, the best are the minority. The mavericks. The rebels. The square pegs in round holes. The dropouts. The freaks. The misfits.

(In spite of the fact that "democracy" subtly assert otherwise ... to be amongst "the majority" isn't necessarily to be, to have chosen, to have "said," to have "thought," or, to have done, "the best.")

Intelligence is Effortless

I once met this good-looking potential-mother-to-my-unborn-kids.

While chatting, I told her about how much I like "smart" women. And that I doubt that I would "start a family" with a not-so-smart woman. For I do not want kids who will "do" grade three thrice.

Anyways, she hoped for "a next time." So when we parted ways, she hinted for yours truly to ask her for her numbers. Which I did. ... All in the name of avoiding yet another "heartbroken" woman.

And because I told her that I think that smart women are the new black; she tried to 'act' all intelligent on me. And she went something like, "Zero oh three, square root of forty-nine, one plus two, seven, wan-wan ... " Talk about a fat person trying to act skinny!

("Intelligence" is a way of thinking; not a way of carrying oneself.)

The Speaker, the Spoken, and, the Spoken To

When in a conversation, ... do people 'speak' because someone is listening? Do people 'listen' merely because someone is speaking?

When a speaker speaks, ... who benefits the most? The speaker or whoever that consumes whatever that's spoken? Well, depending on what is being said, "the spoken" is a gift to "the spoken to."

(Seeing that, "the spoken" was known by the speaker, before the speaker spoke. In the same way that, before a tweet is read, the tweet was known by the twitterer, before the twitterer tweeted.)

The Untold Social Classes

Though the world has over "six and half billion" people; when we leave the "depth of our pockets" out of the equation, we are only divisible into 4 social classes. Below are the 'untold' social classes:

--- Normal people ---

They would rather strive to walk faster; than to dream of flying.

These people hardly fail; because they rarely take risks.

They are induced by the predictability and the comfort of a salary.

They make 'the majority.' On that account, democracy gives them the "power" to give "their power" away.

They see their qualifications as a sign to stop seeking knowledge.

They forever overestimate how much what they think of the third class, matters to the third class.

They are satisfied with consuming and producing average things.

They looooooooooooove telling the third class to be "... realistic."

They think that taking the road not travelled is "... immature."

Without this kind of people, trends would not exist. Because they passionately salute, and blindly worship, looking like other people.

They ~~usually~~ always leave the world the way that they found it.

They "owe" what they foolishly think that they "own."

They'd rather be wrong with everyone than risk being right alone.

--- Stupid people ---

Within this class there are two types: scientists who are expected to master art — and artists who are — expected to master science.

These 'stupid' people are the second most misunderstood beings.

--- Crazy people ---

These are my favourite type of people. The most 'misunderstood.'

This class is made of people who fail to entertain what is; because they are busy 'imagining' what could be. Amongst these "crazy" people were "out of their minds" people like the Wright Brothers.

Two brothers who were 'crazy enough' to believe that they could assemble pieces of metal and then fly people between continents.

Although all classes share this "destination," those who are in the first class are already here. May their souls ~~rest~~ "... live in peace."

Enslaved by Freedom

A creative is free to come up with whatever; but she must remain within the brief. A writer is free to write whatever; but he mustn't exceed, say, 800 words. Plus, ... he must remain within the topic.

An artist is free to paint whatever; but it must fit inside the canvas. A marketer is free to publish whatever; but it must remain within marketing. A pastor is free to say whatever; but it must be 'godly.'

A reporter is free to report whatever; but it must fit within the bulletin. A lover is free to say whatever; but it must be "lovely." An entertainer is free to do whatever; but it must be "entertaining."

A boxer is free to go wherever; but he must remain inside the ring.

A prostitute is free to "sleep with" whoever; but that "whoever" must have at least sixty rands. A polygamist is free to sleep with whoever; but it must be with one of his thirty-five "other halves."

(A comic is free to say whatever; but it must be funny. An employee is free to go wherever -- but she must be in a cubicle by 8 a.m.)

o°

The Beginning.

"Judge me all you want,
just keep the verdict to yourself."

— **Unknown**

Mokokoma Mokhonoana is a philosopher // a social entrepreneur // a creative with mastery of visual communication // An Occasional Failure™

He finds the road ~~less~~ not travelled irresistible.

He is a branding, copywriting, visual communication, philosophy, and, marketing aficionado.

He foolishly believes in things that the majority of the people would regard as "... unrealistic."

He asserts that you (yes, "you!") are a genius.

He has more books than ex-girlfriends. And, he would rather be ~~left~~ wrong alone; than be right with "everybody" else. He sort of hates trends.

He is forever challenging conventional wisdom.

He thinks that "failure" is underrated and that fear is overrated. He religiously practices "minimalism" in everything that he does, or, creates.

He continues to "rant" about "random" things on his official website: **www.mokokoma.com**

Other published writings

To browse other books and essays by Mokokoma, visit *www.mokokoma.com* (each book or essay is listed with links to <u>some</u> retailers from whom you can buy it).

Be one of the first to know

For the most convenient and less noisy way to follow Mokokoma's work, simply subscribe to his newsletter at *www.bit.ly/mokokoma*. Other than an occasional link to his new book, essay, cartoon, or design, his newsletters are made up of nothing but his new aphorisms, which, if you subscribe, you will receive *a week or two before he shares them anywhere*. Your email address will never be shared with anyone, and you can unsubscribe at any time. The maximum number of newsletters you will receive in a month is 4; the minimum is zero.

Liked a few things in this book?

If you found this book worthy of your time, please consider leaving a review, even if it is only a-sentence-or-two long. That seemingly insignificant gesture will immensely help Mokokoma and, more importantly, some, many, or even most of the people who your review will have convinced to read this book.

Printed in Great Britain
by Amazon

69478578R10140